A gift for

_____

Presented by

_____

blessed

living a grateful life

blessed

Ellen Michaud

Best You
from **Reader's Digest**

New York, NY

FOR READER'S DIGEST
Copy Editor: Barbara Booth
Project Designer: Elizabeth Tunnicliffe
Editorial Intern: Kylie Lacey
Senior Art Director: George McKeon
Executive Editor, Trade Publishing: Dolores York
Associate Publisher, Trade Publishing: Rosanne McManus
President and Publisher, Trade Publishing: Harold Clarke

Library of Congress Cataloging-in-Publication Data
Michaud, Ellen.
  Blessed : living a grateful life / Ellen Michaud.
     p. cm.
  ISBN 978-1-60652-192-2
  1. Women--Conduct of life--Anecdotes. 2. Gratitude. I. Title. II. Title: Living a grateful life.
  BJ1610.M53 2011
  179'.9--dc22
                              2010035510

Cover photograph: Shutterstock/Smith&Smith
Interior photographs: iStockphoto
Illustrations: iStockphoto/LittleLion Studio

We are committed to both the quality of our products and the service we provide to our
customers. We value your comments, so please feel free to contact us.

          Best You Books
          The Reader's Digest Association, Inc.
          Adult Trade Publishing
          44 S. Broadway
          White Plains, NY 10601

For more Reader's Digest products and information, visit our website:

          www.rd.com (in the United States)
          www.readersdigest.ca (in Canada)

Printed in the United States of America

1 3 5 7 9 10 8 6 4 2

For Wayne, whose constant love and fierce honesty have kept me grounded, given me strength, and made all things possible.

For Matthew, whose sweet spirit, loving heart, and penetrating intellect have blessed my life with joy.

For Edna, whose thoughtful insights, caring heart, and faithful life have helped me become the kind of woman I want to be.

And for all those who help us see the blessings of God in every moment. In the midst of darkness, it is they who help us see the Light.

Contents

Foreword

When I asked Ellen Michaud to write an online column called "Blessed" for the millions of *Curves* health club members around the globe, I wanted her to look around at the lives of women everywhere and uncover the everyday blessings women experience—the ones that we're all too busy to see because we're working, running errands, and caring for our families.

I knew that Ellen, with her talent and her heart, could do it. As she has shown in the pages of *Reader's Digest* magazine, *Better Homes and Gardens, Prevention* magazine, the *New York Times,* and my own *diane* magazine, she has that precious gift of being able to see the simple things that bring great joy to our complicated lives.

What's more, she sees those things, then turns around and shows us how each of us is a blessing to others. Most of us don't see ourselves as "good enough" or "doing enough," but Ellen does. She sees us how we really are.

In the following pages, Ellen's vision will help you see the blessing you are to your family, friends, coworkers, neighbors, even the global community—and she'll help you see the blessings that surround you.

In my own life, I've been blessed with an amazing faith that gives me the strength to handle life's challenges, an amazing company of people at *Curves* who have my back, and an amazing family that offers me joy, laughter, tears, forgiveness, and everlasting love.

As Ellen likes to remind me, blessings flow.

Diane Heavin
Cofounder of *Curves*

Introduction ————————

Sitting in an old Adirondack chair outside my cottage high in the mountains of Vermont, I simply can't move. The late afternoon sun has baked every inch of my body into the chair's worn wood. Polished by generations of women sliding back to catch their breath or sliding forward to pull a child onto their laps, the chair holds me as firmly in place as the sun splashing through the trees.

I know I should get up and do any one of a zillion things—wash the dog, wash the dishes, wash the windows, wash my hair—but it just isn't going to happen. No one's throwing up, no one's starving, no one needs to be picked up, dropped off, or shuttled from one end of the planet to the other, and no employer is close enough to demand my energy or a moment of my life.

So here I sit, eyes almost closed, not moving, deeply relaxed. I'm not even really writing these words—just kind of letting them flow.

But somewhere deep inside my chest there's a twinge of unease, a little ripple of something not quite right. Sitting in the sun is not my natural state. Like most women, I nurture whole villages of people, starting with my family, then extending out to my neighborhood, church, town, state, nation, even the world. There's a woman at my church whose husband lost his job, a neighbor whose husband was diagnosed with cancer, a child in Kenya who needs a home. And every inch of the globe seems bound and determined to act out of the meanest, smallest, most violent part of human nature.

How can I sit in the sun? It's a question every woman asks. How can I sit in the sun when so many people need me? How can I take the time for a workout? How can I meet friends for lunch?

But just as I'm about to jump up and leap back into the life stream of ATMs, grocery stores, and soccer fields, a chickadee sends its long, slow call searching through the woods around me.

"Chee, che-che-che-che-chee..."

The sweetness catches my attention. In a moment, the tightness within my chest eases, and I open my eyes to scan the tall pines around the clearing in which my cottage sits.

The call comes again, solitary, its beauty capturing my turbulent spirit, filling my heart with light, and—how?—the understanding that sitting here, resting and listening as generations of women before me have done, is what connects me to what's important in life. Because when the spirit is still, the mind quiet, the body at peace, the whispers of God are everywhere, and the joy of Presence is within.

This book is like my chair. It offers an opportunity to hear the sweet sounds of a single chickadee. It captures our turbulent spirits, fills our hearts with light, and holds the understanding that pausing for just a moment to rest and listen, to think and reflect, as generations of women before us have done, is what connects us to what's important.

It allows us a quiet space and a moment of clarity in which to examine and celebrate our relationships with family and friends. To look at the meaning and purpose of our lives. To think about how we might make a difference in the world. To renew, refresh, and even reinvent who we are.

Because when the spirit is still, the mind quiet, the body at peace, the whispers of God are everywhere.

We are so blessed.

A Quiet Space

We need a deeper quiet and listening that permeates our whole way of being. We need to live a life that quiets down enough to be able to hear that still, small voice.

—Sandra Cronk, in *A Lasting Gift: The Journal and Selected Writings of Sandra L. Cronk*

A Time to Listen

In a world that has too many abrupt changes—in places, people, and lives—the breath between summer and fall offers a gentle transition that slows us down and gives us time to listen to our lives.

Taking the last swallow of morning coffee, I plunked the empty mug in the sink, picked up my gardening gloves from beside the back door and headed outside with the dog.

The sun was just beginning to appear over the thick pines surrounding my yard, and the garden was still in shade. A neighboring partridge whirred through the underbrush on his way home, and Rufus, my intrepid West Highland terrier, shot off to investigate.

Chuckling, I turned my attention to the garden. A couple of weeks ago, it was beautiful. A bouquet of tall sunflowers in the middle had been surrounded on all four sides by successive plantings of lettuce, beans, and carrots throughout the cool Vermont summer.

Since then, however, chickadees and titmice had stripped the sunflowers bare, and the shorter days had discouraged the beans from flowering. The carrots were still snuggled in their burrows, of course, but the lettuce—Little Gems, my husband's favorite romaine—were starting to get that translucent look that signifies impending wilt or incipient bolt.

I pulled a big, woven basket out from its hiding place beneath a tree and began to pull up the beans and any errant weeds. In half an hour, the basket was full and an exhausted Westie had returned to sprawl in the cool grass beside me. He had assured the family's safety from marauding partridges and was now content to lie down, ears pricked, and listen to the wind.

I finished weeding, then sat on the grass beside him. "That old partridge outfox you again?" I asked. I ruffled the dog's coat, inhaled the sweet morning air, and listened with him.

This is my favorite time of year. It's a deep, slow breath between late summer vacations, soccer sign-ups, and early fall chores such as taking out the screens, painting the house, making applesauce, and preparing the garden for winter.

It lasts only moments. But in a world that has too many abrupt changes—in places, people, and lives—the breath between summer and fall offers a gentle transition that slows us down and gives us time to listen to our lives.

It gives us time to notice the Canada geese arriving on my neighbor's pond at dusk with a feathery splash and, like good houseguests, taking themselves off immediately after an early morning breakfast.

It gives us time to notice the hummingbirds gathering in the clearing as they tank up on nectar from the feeder, then take off like small feathered emissaries headed for Central and South America.

How do they know when it's time to go? How do they know where they'll find food? How will they keep track of their children? Do they simply take off and have faith that what they need will be provided?

Do I? Could I just hop in the car and head south without credit cards and reservations? How would my life be different if I did?

I looked down at Rufus, lying content in the morning sun. And I listened more deeply.

The Perfect Apple Pie

In tough times and a turbulent world, a quiet space
knits generations of women together.

Driving down the dirt road that leads to Shelburne Orchards, a wild tumble of delicate Queen Anne's lace and dried grasses brush either side of the car. Newly bailed hay is scattered across nearby fields, cornstalks rustle in the breeze, and cows munch their way through the last of the pasture grass.

October is a special time in Vermont, especially here along Lake Champlain. Light reflects off the lake, touches the hills with fire, and envelops our farms in a warm golden glow found nowhere else in the world. Wood smoke begins to scent the air, Canada geese honk their way south, and buffalo plaids emerge from cedar-lined closets.

The first frost is imminent, and most of us have already put our gardens to bed for the winter. Spinach, beans, and peas are safely tucked into Ziploc bags in the freezer. Pumpkins are in the cellar. Tomatoes have been canned and now line pantry shelves in rich ruby reds that glow with the summer. Carrots are tucked safely underground where they'll continue to keep perfectly—covered with straw against the chill of early snows—right through Thanksgiving.

The one thing remaining to be harvested are apples, and it's the apples I'm after today. Their rich scent drifts through the trees as I turn onto the orchard's road and pull up next to the farm stand. Macoun,

Mutsu, empire, and golden delicious should all be ready for picking, along with the remaining crop of McIntosh. I wave to the couple weighing apples at the stand, grab a couple of canvas boat bags from the back of my car, and head into the apple trees.

As I wander through the orchard, the scent reminds me of the smells that floated through my grandmother's kitchen as she and I made apple pies and tarts when I was little.

I'd stand on a red-and-white stool next to her at the counter as she donned a bib apron, reached into a cupboard for her big ceramic bowl, and pulled a well-used pastry blender out of the drawer. A big can of vegetable shortening—always Crisco—sat waiting on the countertop, and it wasn't long before she'd combined flour and shortening with a few drops of water to form a dough. Then she'd turn the whole thing out onto a floured counter and shape it with her maple rolling pin. *Fold, fold, turn, roll.*

Eventually the crust would be dropped into a glass pie plate, and we'd turn our attention to the apples. Each one was peeled and cored by hand, then sliced with a paring knife and tossed into a ceramic bowl with sugar, cinnamon, and a pinch of ground nutmeg. I got to stir. Then it sat on the counter while we stood, side by side at the sink, and cleaned measuring spoons, cups, and bowls.

Once the rich, dark apple syrup formed, my grandmother would slip the mixture gently into the pie plate, dot the apples with butter, and top them with a second crust. Then I'd carved my initials into the top crust to vent the steam, and she'd slip the pie into the oven.

As the pie baked, my grandmother and I would sit at the kitchen table to have tea. The grandfather clock—a tall case clock made in England sometime before 1756—would tick in a corner, steadily counting out the seconds, minutes, and hours of life, while a family of sparrows nested and chirped outside the kitchen window.

For a young girl who had traveled the world with her family since she was born, these were precious moments. My father was always immersed in politics and military budgets. My mother with the social role a military wife was required to play. There was no one to listen to a young girl's chatter, to help her make sense of the world, to reassure her that, yes, in a chaotic world in turbulent times, there were still quiet places where some things—particularly apples, pies, and grandmothers—never changed.

Now, as I pick the apples at Shelburne Orchards, then go home to pull my grandmother's cookbook from the bookshelf and her paint-chipped pastry blender from the drawer, I move seamlessly into that quiet space that knits generations of women together—a space that, in tough times and a turbulent world, gives each of us a calm, quiet center in which to grow as we wait out the storm.

I am so blessed.

By the Sea

*I close my eyes and feel the warm sun begin to
slow the focused determination that has kept me moving
ahead for months, maybe even years.*

Lifting up a cup of freshly brewed coffee from my favorite café along the rugged California coast, my eyes follow the curve of the purple Santa Monica Mountains as they plunge into the sea. Seagulls skim the surf, looking for clams, a misty sun blesses the waves with sparkling silver threads, and white sand softly warms my bare feet.

I've come here to heal.

Exhaustion curls around my edges. It slows my mind, drops pouches under my eyes, weights my step. The cause is nothing more than what every woman experiences on a daily basis—a demanding job, aging parents, stressed kids, unexpected illness, an always-there mortgage, and a husband re-evaluating his life as he carefully negotiates the midlife transition. Where is he going? Where has be been? Did he accomplish what he set out to do? To be? Has he made the world a better place? The questions are exhausting, the struggle hard to watch.

Sipping the rich black Urth coffee, I close my eyes and feel the warm sun begin to slip around the exhaustion and slow the focused determination that has kept me moving ahead for months, maybe even years. I stroll back from the beach to my cottage, settle into an old wicker chair, and let the sun's warmth separate me into layers.

It always amazes me what women do. If a child wakes in the night, we're there. If a woman in the community needs shelter, we take her in. If a friend loses a mate, we answer her phone, feed her children, and help her bury her husband. If an elderly aunt gets vague and forgetful, we round her up, bring her home, park her in a comfortable chair beside a sunny window, and make her a cup of tea. If children half a world away need shelter, we gather our friends, pool our money, and do whatever it takes to raise a roof, build some walls, and make sure each child has a warm blanket and a safe space in which to play.

We never say no—and we rarely take time for ourselves. A hairdresser appointment once every month or so, a massage tucked in here and there, or a quick walk as we pick up fresh veggies and milk at the Wild Oats or Kroger's or Hannaford's.

We never take time to just sit in the sun.

An odd bird squawks over my head, pulling me out of my reverie. Its head is a ruffled ocean blue that streaks back over its shoulders, eventually darkening and blending into rusty orange streaks below its throat and over its chest. It perches on the wicker chair next to me and tilts its head first one way, then another as it studies the overhanging roof of the cottage where I'm staying.

I watch as it flies up under the overhang, disappears for a minute, then flies to a nearby tree. Back and forth it goes for a dozen trips. I'm not sure what it's doing, but it's certainly working hard. It may have a nest tucked under the overhang, filled with babies, or perhaps up in the tree.

Eventually, however, it settles onto a branch, flutters its feathers in the sun, throws back its head, and begins a song of the most unexpected sweetness.

Once again, I close my eyes. But this time I listen to what I'm hearing.

Summer in a Jar

Vegetables freshly tugged from the earth, Jerseys grazing in the pasture, a back porch, and a friend mark the edge of autumn.

Driving down the two-lane road that wanders past tall rows of ready-to-harvest cornstalks and freshly mown fields dotted with bales of hay, I watch carefully for the unmarked driveway at Orb Weaver Farm.

Built over the past quarter century by two women on a hundred-acre hillside not far from the shores of Vermont's Lake Champlain, the farm is justly famed among local children for its sweet-faced Jersey cows and among local chefs for its prizewinning cheese.

But today it's not the cheese that draws me down the road. It's the end-of-summer cornucopia of peppers, tomatoes, and onions that my friend Marjorie has harvested from her garden—and which I intend to turn into what I know, on good authority, is one of the finest salsas in the near world. It's based on a recipe my friend Kathy developed with her mom some 10 years ago, and even here in the Vermont countryside where every woman makes a superb salsa, the first questioning nibble of *this* salsa at any church potluck or community supper brings raised eyebrows and an appreciative murmur.

Spotting the driveway, I pull off the road and swing into an out-of-the-way area beside the 200-year-old farmhouse. Marjorie and the farm's dog, a friendly Rhodesian something-or-other, wander over to greet me.

"So you made it?" asks Marjorie with a sweet smile. "Come around back—I've got your stuff on the porch. See what you think."

Strolling around a corner of the house, I stop dead. What I think is that I've wandered into the Garden of Eden, and my intention to toss the produce into my creaky Subaru, run home, turn it into salsa as fast as I can, and get on to other things withers on the vine.

Instead, I look out at the rumpled fields stretching across the fertile valley, take a deep breath, and inhale the heavy, rich smell of freshly picked tomatoes, the piquant scent of peppers, and the primordial aroma of onions not long from the earth.

"Oh-h-h…" I say softly.

Marjorie looks at me in understanding. There's something about vegetables freshly tugged from the earth that speaks to the soul. "Sit down," she invites, and perches companionably on the porch.

Looking over at the sweet Jersey girls grazing in the pasture, then over toward her partner Marian, working the far fields with her tractor, I realize that there's a natural rhythm here that's far out of sync with cell phone and Blackberry, laptop or broadband.

Marjorie and I slide easily into conversation, as do women everywhere, and eventually Marian's tractor bumps over the ground toward the barn, stops, then rumbles into the farm's deep silence as she climbs to the ground and comes over to say hello. Clearly, she's busy as a cat with a new litter of kittens. But as she reaches out her hand to greet me, I realize that here, where the work it takes to run a farm, manage a herd, make cheese, and run a business is never done, there is always time to greet a neighbor, talk about the weather, and inquire into the nature of things. I slide into the rhythm of it without missing a beat.

Long after I've said my good-byes and left the farm, as I slip the skins from Marjorie's tomatoes and chop her onions and peppers, the resolve grows that, every year, I'll take one day at the edge of autumn, visit the farm, make salsa, and try to capture summer in a jar.

The Quiet Time

*With roads covered by several feet of new snow, a roaring fire
in the woodstove, and a stack of seed catalogs on the coffee table,
I'm content to curl up in front of the fire and dream.*

Outside my cottage high in the mountains of Vermont, snow is piled up to the window boxes. The road that cuts through the forest is bordered by a 4-foot wall of snow built by a neighbor's early morning plow, the power's out, and narrow paths shoveled here and there from cottage to woodpile, cottage to mailbox, and even cottage to compost pile are almost obscured by several feet of new snow.

As I check to see if the phone works, the frenzied bark of a West Highland white terrier knifes through the frigid air, and I realize that even in this white, arctic world, one of my crazy dogs is racing along the paths hidden from view—probably in hot pursuit of a seed-munching squirrel. Figuring I'd better get outdoors before the short-legged hunter wannabe flounders in a snowbank, I slip my feet into boots, pull on a red down vest and some serious mittens, fill two plastic pitchers full of sunflower seeds, and then head out.

The birdfeeders hanging from the red pines have clearly been doing a boffo business. Chickadees, woodpeckers, nuthatches, titmice— the silence of my clearing is constantly blessed by the soft *thwwp!* of feathered wings as the birds explode into flying windmills leaving or landing on a feeder. And they don't seem to mind me. They twirl past my shoulder to perch on a branch about 18 inches from my nose.

I have even gotten into the habit of talking to them as I open and fill their feeders. "Good morning, pretty one," I greet the chickadee who has decided to supervise breakfast. She cocks her head first one way, then another, and watches closely as I fill the feeders—almost as though she is deciding whether or not I have lined up the breakfast china just so.

I must have done it right, because even as I'm tightening the cap on the last feeder, she softly brushes my cheek with her whirring wings and lands on the feeder with an excited "chirr-UP!"

Chuckling, I round up the Westie and head back inside.

After feeding the dogs, I pour a hot mug of coffee and settle into my reading chair in the tiny living room. With roads covered by several feet of new snow, a roaring fire in the woodstove, and a stack of seed catalogs on the coffee table, I'm content to curl up in front of the fire and dream of the garden I've yet to plant.

Gardening up here in the mountains is tough. Our growing season is short, our soil thin, and mesclun-loving deer plentiful. So it takes a lot of thought to get just the right plants—or so I tell myself as I begin to page through catalogs from The Cook's Garden, Gardener's Supply Company, Seeds of Change, Peaceful Valley Farm Supply, and a dozen others from a dozen other companies in a dozen other states.

But as my mind wanders through fields of sweet, organic corn, beds of deep green broccoli, and amid planters overflowing with parsley and thyme, I realize that these catalogs are simply an excuse to let myself dream. To ignore my six-day-a-week work schedule. To ignore the dishes piled high in the sink. To ignore the bills waiting to be paid. To not go anywhere. To not call anyone, anywhere, about anything.

It's a space in which to breathe.

The Storm

The wild energy and undisciplined power that spills from
the skies can make unexpected revelations.

The storm roared across the mountains ripping 50-foot pines from the ground. Sugar maples were splintered, apple trees stripped of their bark, poplars tossed across roads. Delicate birches bent toward the earth, covered with swirling snow.

As the wind howled and shook my cottage high in the mountains, Rufus—the rugged West Highland terrier who shares my life—lifted his head. Ears up, he listened to the sounds outside, identifying and evaluating the nuances of each. The wild keening of the wind, the edgy whisper of icy snow, the snap of branches, the soft boom of a falling tree.

He didn't like any of it. Getting up from the warm hearth in front of the woodstove, he padded to the door and sniffed along the bottom. His nose studied the situation until he'd confirmed that no attack from the outside was imminent. But he didn't go back to the fire. As one tree after another fell—some, literally, scraping my cottage walls—he stayed alert, eyes on the door, ready to protect his family.

I love storms. I love the wild energy and undisciplined power that spills from the skies. I like the unpredictability that turns the world upside down. And as long as no creatures are hurt and I'm tucked inside my own warm nest, I love the sharp scent of cold air, the crystalline purity of snow, the deep silence of the woods underneath the storm.

Sipping a hot cup of tea as I snuggle into an oversized chair by the fire, I surrender control of my life to the storm and relax into the realization that no phone can ring, no TV can demand my attention, no e-mail can appear in front of my eyes. Today, in this moment and in this place, I am quite simply not responsible for anything. Not picking up groceries. Not dropping off a child. Not figuring out the income tax.

Instead I watch as the chickadees flit back and forth under the protective branches of feathery hemlocks and voles sculpt long white mounds as they tunnel beneath the snow. I watch as a 1,000-pound dark chocolate–colored moose steps through the snow searching for a frozen patch of greens—and hold my breath as a magnificent white snowy owl drops silently from a branch to hunt unsuspecting prey beneath the snow.

I live in a magical place. God is woven into the fabric of life here on the mountain, but like most of us who are overwhelmed with work, dishes, laundry, errands, and the zillion and one other tasks of daily life, I simply don't stop long enough to pay attention or be nurtured by the experience. Instead, I tear through the day, checking stuff off my to-do list, then fall into bed exhausted.

Getting up to light candles as dusk darkens the room, I hear more trees falling in the forest. They are close, and Rufus is restless. But the cottage is warm, the dogs are safe, a rich fish chowder is simmering on the woodstove, and I am reminded of what's important.

We are blessed.

Finding Meaning

It's not about you.

—Rick Warren, pastor of Saddleback Community Church,
in *The Purpose Driven Life*

Welcome Home

In an instant the Airbus 321 became deathly quiet.

Gently gliding over the desert as we descended from 35,000 feet toward the coastal lights of Los Angeles International Airport, the passengers around me on U.S. Airways Flight 893 from Philadelphia began to collect the water bottles, shoes, books, and headsets that had been stashed around the Airbus 321 during our five-hour flight.

Pulling up plastic window shades to peer out past our own shadowed reflections, we could see that except for an abstract splash of stars above and a grid of streetlights below, the night was pitch-black. Ahead was the darkness of the Pacific, behind the darkness of the desert. Only here, as we slid seamlessly out of the blackness toward the explosion of runway lights ahead, could we see the earth with any clarity.

Awkwardly, the captain's voice broke our silence. "We have a situation here, folks," he began.

In an instant the Airbus became deathly quiet.

"We'll be landing in a few moments, and I'm just going to ask you to keep your seats when I open the door. I…"

He hesitated.

"You may have noticed three young men riding with us today, two of whom are in uniform. They're escorting three soldiers who are riding with us downstairs. So I'd just like you to remain seated and let these guys get off the plane first to accord them some privacy. I'm an ex-military pilot myself, and—it doesn't matter what your politics are—I know you'll respect what they have to do."

Downstairs? I looked around in confusion.

Across the aisle, an older woman who had been reading the latest Tom Clancy thriller closed her eyes and let the book fall to her lap.

Next to her, a businesswoman who had been running charts and graphs on her laptop during the entire flight gently closed her screen, folded her hands on top of the quiet computer, and bowed her head.

My seatmate, a young systems engineer from Erie on his way to Disneyland, reached out a hand to his young wife and gently squeezed her fingers.

Suddenly, I realized what the pilot had meant.

Gradually, the small sounds of sorting, stuffing, and repacking returned to the cabin, but quietly, softly, without the anticipation or urgency they'd had. We were all thinking of the three young men riding silently beneath our feet.

My seatmate turned and looked down at me searchingly. Just minutes before, we had been discussing the war in the Middle East and questioning why we were there.

It was an uncomfortable question for someone like me who had grown up an army brat—one of those strong, friendly, competent and competitive kids who had been able to leap tall buildings in a single bound. I knew all about protocols, perks, and pecking orders. I knew how to strip down a rifle, climb a cargo net, organize a base rummage sale, sneak off post past the MPs, not read "TOP SECRET" documents on my dad's desk, and dodge under helicopter rotors when Santa landed every Christmas.

The daughter of two U.S. Army captains, I also knew men and women who had pulled us through World War II, flown missions over Korea and then into Laos, and, finally, the men who had slid into the jungles of Vietnam and home to 30-some years of nightmares and a battle with the bottle.

Patriotism was a given, service a life's work, sacrifice a matter of course.

But tonight, on the quiet inbound flight to LA, the sacrifices made by the young men below had turned the 185 of us on board into pall-bearers. I was overwhelmed with grief.

The Airbus slowly slipped to the ground and, with the pilot's tender care for his quiet cargo, gently touched the runway. The aircraft remained deathly quiet as it taxied to the gate. Then, as the three young soldiers sitting in the midst of us unbuckled their seatbelts and stood to retrieve their bags from the overhead storage compartment, the sound of one person clapping broke the silence. Another joined in, then another, and another, until, as the young men walked up the aisle, the entire aircraft resounded with the intensity and passion of 185 Americans who held their soldiers in love and respect.

The tears slid down my face. Some of us on board supported the war; others strenuously opposed it. But in the final analysis, every single person on that plane was an American, who held the men walking up that aisle in their hearts, and in their prayers.

"Welcome home," I said silently to the soldiers downstairs. *"Welcome home."*

A Faith Community

As it has for nearly two centuries, a simple country church sits
in a profound stillness rich with a sense of Presence.

As I carefully drive across the tumbling Baldwin Creek and turn up a
dirt road toward the 200-year-old church high in the Vermont mountains, an early morning frost sparkles across meadows stuffed with spiky
milkweed, exuberant goldenrod, and gone-to-seed Queen Anne's lace.
Trees line the road as it twists up the hill through the woods, and a rich,
golden sun turns the swirling piles of leaves along the road into bits of
maple fire.

Swinging into the clearing in which the church sits, I turn off the
engine and listen. Far off across the hills to the north, the faint buzz
of a chainsaw tells me that someone's cutting wood. To the south, a
dog barks.

But here there is no sound. As it has for nearly two centuries, this
simple country church sits in a profound stillness rich with a sense
of Presence.

There are too few moments like this in my life. Instead, like women
everywhere, I'm usually frantically running from one place to another as
I pick up groceries, drop off pets, get to work, swing by schools, and run
through the bank's drive-in.

But once in a while when some chore or another brings me here
alone to weed the flower beds or to make sure there's enough wood
stacked in the woodshed, the silence allows me to hear—to sense—that

still, small voice that whispers the truth about what's important in life. Like the joyous sound of a brook that's always present but obscured by the larger and louder sounds of a fast and angry world, that voice expands in silence and fills my mind with thoughts of the remarkable people who gather here to worship.

Grabbing my gardening gloves and trowel out of the backseat, I think of Jane, an elderly woman who has been known to march across our well-trimmed lawn, pause beside a car stopped to watch our festivities, open up a conversation with its passengers, then lead them into the paths of righteousness before the driver can get his foot off the brake.

I think of Peggy's softly ferocious caring as she quizzes Jane and her husband, Sam, to make sure they've been eating well, dressing warmly, getting to their doctor appointments, and getting phone calls from their globe-trotting children.

I think of Joy, who always comes early to make sure a fire has been built in the woodstove, and of Greg, her beloved husband, who carefully checks to make sure the mice haven't taken over the vestibule.

I think of Kerry, who's always ready to tighten a step so our old folks won't trip or hold a flower sale so we can pay the awe-inspiring insurance bill that arrives regular as frost this time of year.

And I think of Jill, who so recently lost her brother. Of Robert, who's lost his mom. Of Jim, who's fighting to save his. Of Elise, who misses her Ted. Of Tim and Marie and Douglas and Patty, who…

By the time I've finished weeding and pruning and thinking, piles of weeds and branches are around my feet, my heart is alive with love, and I realize that this small community of faith—this tiny little church halfway up a mountain and filled with ordinary people—is a tiny microcosm of all that's right with the world.

And that's a blessing.

A Vermont Thanksgiving

Things are a little different this year.

OK. The turkey's in the oven. Potatoes are on the stove. Stuffing's cooling on the counter. Whacking the shelled pecans with a wooden mallet on my cutting board, I mentally take inventory for our Thanksgiving dinner:

- Tofurky for my vegan husband: ✓
- Mushrooms for the gravy: ✓
- Cranberry sauce for my elderly aunt: ✓
- Carrots freshly pulled from the garden: ✓
- Table set with my grandmother's linens and china: ✓
- Totally tacky pilgrim squirrel salt 'n pepper shakers on the table (don't ask): ✓

Oops. Forgot to make the applesauce. Hurriedly, I grab a half-dozen McIntoshes from the apple bin and place them on the counter. There. Now I won't forget them.

Picking up my wooden mallet once again, I think about the meal ahead. It's a little bit different this year. The turkey's smaller, the stuffing's made from leftover stale bread I've been tossing in the freezer for a month, I'm omitting the chocolate favors, skipping the elaborate centerpiece from the florist, and substituting an apple pie for the southern pecan pie that's been a tradition in our home for generations.

With pecans costing $7.99 a pound—and with my propensity for making hefty pies—I've decided our bank accounts and waistlines can do without the pecan pie. Instead, freshly picked, peeled, and cored Vermont apples, a bit of sugar, a few chunks of butter, half a teaspoon of nutmeg, a pinch of ground cloves, an egg to hold it all together, and a sprinkle of crushed pecans on top with some brown sugar will do very nicely. Total cost: about $3.00.

Whacking my last nut, I toss the mallet in the sink and brush the nuts from my cutting board into a small prep bowl. A quarter cup of brown sugar, a quarter cup of bread crumbs, butter to moisten, and the handful of pecans I've crushed are quickly mixed in and sprinkled over the pie.

Done. Into the oven it goes. After setting the timer, I pull on a sweater, slip into a pair of warm moccasins, and take a huge mug of tea out to the deck.

Fall in Vermont is incredible. The sun turns leaves scattered over our roads into maple fire. The rye grasses that are planted each fall to nourish the fields cover the ground in that luminescent green that make most people think of Ireland. The rich brown earth of our cornfields reflects years of care with organic fertilizers. And the meadows! Wild grasses, gone-to-seed Queen Anne's lace, mini crab apples from a wild tree, milkweed with their dried pods bursting with white silk threads, wildflowers dried on the stalk...

Sipping my tea, I look out over the incredible richness that surrounds me. The woodpile that reflects my husband's determination to keep us warm. The garden I planted to keep us fed.

I finish my tea and grab a basket to gather grasses, pods, and crab apples for a centerpiece.

Yes, things are a little different this year. But the house is warm. There's food on the table. My son will be home. And my friend Joy has survived breast cancer.

Some days, it's all in your perspective. The blessings flow.

Cleaning House

Who knows what's at the bottom of the basement stairs.

I couldn't put it off any longer.

The garden was flourishing, the house was clean, the dogs had been fed, and I had just finished work on my latest book. Sighing, I knew it was time.

It was July.

It was hot.

That meant it was time to descend into the coolness of our basement and clean it. Time to sweep the sawdust created by the various saws, drills, and assorted toys my husband uses to cut down trees, cut up boards, and build me everything from window boxes to bookshelves. Time to vacuum up a year's worth of cat fur. Time to untangle cords, restack bins, and shore up sagging shelves. Time to pull out the washing machine and dryer and—finally!—find all those missing socks.

I was gonna hate every minute.

Feeling thoroughly disgruntled, I opened the cupboard under the kitchen sink and hauled out buckets, brushes, rags, dusters, and a huge bottle of concentrated citrus cleaner. The vacuum and assorted brushes and brooms were already in the basement.

I began with the basement stairs. After giving the cat warning that a shower of dried mud tramped up the stairs from the basement's garden door was about to become airborne in the vicinity of her litter box, I swept 12 months of sand, dirt, and ground stone toward the darkness below.

Following it down, I dumped my cleaning tools and products on the cellar floor, turned on the basement vacuum, and sucked up every bit of dirt I could find. Then I picked up the dust-attracting magic wands I'd bought at the supermarket and proceeded to remove every bit of dust, sawdust, and spiderweb I could see. I dealt with the cords, bins, and sagging shelves as I went.

By the time I'd worked my way around to the wall beside the garden door, I was filthy. But I had gotten into the ancient rhythm of women who understand the imperatives of nesting and the need for seasonal cleaning. I was no longer disgruntled. Instead, as I slid my magic wand over the old steamer trunk my family had brought from England three generations ago, a kind of gentle silence seemed to settle around me.

On impulse I flipped open the trunk's locks and lifted the lid.

Inside were scrapbooks, wedding invitations, graduation announcements, funeral notices, my son's artwork from nursery school, his baby clothes, my baby clothes, letters from me to my mom in the year before she died, my son's baby book, an elaborately etched bottle of *Dans la Nuit* perfume my mother had brought back from France after World War II, a Portuguese shawl from my honeymoon, and a gazillion family photographs—photos of my dad in uniform, my mother in uniform, photos of my mother's parents on picnics or playing cricket in England, my mother's sister on skis, and one panoramic photo of the SS *Cynthia*, the ship that had brought my mother's parents from England to the United States.

It was a beautiful heritage.

What was not in the trunk, however, were any photos or mementos of my father's family from South Carolina. It was not because they were poor, which they had been, but rather it was because my father's mother, a woman with beautiful blue eyes and long blond hair, had had one of the meanest, most manipulative temperaments on the planet.

She'd constantly belittled my father as a child and had doted on his older brother, which could have something to do with the fact that my father left home at 17, joined the army, and never looked back.

My grandmother came to visit a few times as I was growing up. Although my parents never said an unkind word about her, her behavior told me everything. "Your brother's got better saltshakers than these," she'd sneer at my father over the dinner table. Or to me: "Your cousin Vicki's a lot prettier than you."

That I could forgive—especially since Vicki *was* prettier. What I could not forgive, however, was the fact that my father went to his grave feeling unloved and unwanted by his own mother.

Propelled by faith, I've tried all the tricks that are supposed to help me forgive her. I've researched my grandmother's history and tried to walk a mile in her moccasins. I've thought long and hard about what it might have been like for her to have been the middle child in a family of 13. And I've considered how difficult it must have been to support three children on her own after her husband had died.

But forgiveness is hard. And even as the gentle silence settled comfortingly around me, I couldn't dissolve the anger within that stood between me and forgiveness. I wanted to, but I couldn't. And what did that say about me?

Finally I stepped away from the trunk.

Standing on my tiptoes, I reached for a box high on a nearby shelf, opened it, and removed a yellowed, cracked photo of my father's mother. Without giving it more than a brief glance, I dropped it into the trunk with the rest of my family's history and shut the lid.

That was all I could do today. The rest would come by the grace of God.

Digging in the Past

*In a turbulent world, tending flowers and plants from those
we love strengthens the connections between us.*

Stepping out onto the deck with my morning coffee, I take a deep
breath of the rich, earthy scents that yesterday's rain has left behind and
watch as the sun emerges from behind the pines that shelter my cottage.

It's still cold up here in the Vermont mountains, but already the
chickadees are singing, the doves have returned to coo in the trees, and
the ruffled grouse is beating a fallen log with his wings. His drumming
is directed to the lady grouses in the neighborhood so they'll know that
he's ready, willing, and able to set up housekeeping once again.

Laughing at his determined rhythm, I pull my down vest a little
closer and step carefully off the deck onto the spongy grass.

This is my favorite time of year. The compost pile's still frozen, and
the ground's too wet to work. So instead of heading for the wheel-
barrow and the cache of gardening tools tucked under the kitchen deck,
I wander around the area sipping my coffee.

The Irish mosses under the towering red pines have already begun to
green up, particularly along the path that meanders through the woods.
The poplars' gnarly branches are bursting with soft pussy-willow seed-
pods, buds have formed on my sturdy mountain magnolia, and the
tips of what will soon be crocuses and early daffodils are beginning to
emerge from around the base of a tall pine.

Putting my coffee cup down on a handy tree stump, I reach in my pocket and pull out a small sketch pad and pen to make some notes.

It's been a hard winter, but so far things look good. Turning up the slope toward the edge of the forest, I notice that the pachysandra is starting to lose its stunned I've-been-under-the-snow-for-four-months look and is actually flowering.

The groundcover's resilience amazes me. This particular clump of pachysandra was planted around my family home in Pennsylvania nearly 60 years ago. My aunt tended it, then gave me a few cuttings when I married and moved to my first house. I've moved several times since, and each time, I've left flourishing clumps of pachysandra surrounding my old house and taken a few dozen cuttings with me for the new. The clumps flowering in the snow before me are the latest offspring.

I make a few notes about transplanting some of the new shoots in a few weeks, then wander across the circular pebbled drive toward the stone wall my husband built to separate the driveway from my beds of roses, daylilies, and peonies.

I shift a few stones back into place and search the beds for signs of life. The peonies speak to my heart. I found the first plants beside the back steps at my first house, and, like the pachysandra, I've moved them from house to house until they reached Vermont.

To this day they remind me of Rosalie, the next-door neighbor who took me under her wing when I was pregnant with my first child. I knew as little about caring for a child as I did about caring for a bed of peonies when we first met, but Rosalie showed me the way. The day my husband and I moved in, she turned up with a pitcher of lemonade, a plate of homemade cookies, a heart overflowing with kindness, and the conviction that God had brought us together for a reason. She helped me find a pediatrician, a church, and a diaper service, drove me to the hospital and held my hand through a near miscarriage, and celebrated with my young husband when our baby stayed right where he was supposed to.

Once our baby was born some weeks later, Rosalie showed me how to care for him. And when the peonies began to push up through the cold spring earth, she showed me how to care for them, as well. Today, even though she's hundreds of miles south, as I look out over the peony bed along the stone wall, carefully checking for any of the red shoots from what must now be a hundred different plants, I feel Rosalie's beautiful spirit all around.

In fact, I feel the sweet spirits of many old friends surrounding me as I look around my yard. A junco flits from branch to branch in the lilac bushes my friend Jennifer gave me a couple of years ago, then hops over to the rose of Sharon, my friend Debbie's mom, Betty, gave me a few years before she died. Both Betty and her flowering hedge were tough enough to survive the winter winds on Shelter Island, a tiny cookie of land off Long Island, but Vermont winters are another story. I make a note to ask Debbie for new cuttings next time she visits her mother's old home.

Wandering back toward my abandoned coffee cup, the sense of peace and spiritual connection surrounding me is strong. My friends and I are hundreds and thousands of miles and even whole lifetimes apart. We are separated by time and distance, and death. But every time I loosen the dirt around one of the plants they've given me, every time I snip a perfect blossom or prune a delicate branch, I feel them standing beside me.

I have been so blessed.

Christmas Fire

On Christmas night, men, women, and children come out of the hills and surrounding farms to sing carols, light candles, dream of miracles, and open their hearts to the Presence of God.

As dusk begins to move through the snowy woods surrounding the old Vermont church, I carefully guide my car off the road and into the clearing where the building has nestled for almost 200 years.

Originally built by a group of Quaker farmers, the church is simple—a white two-story clapboard building with tall many-paned windows that look out toward an ancient cemetery and the surrounding trees.

There are only two rooms. One, a long narrow space lined with old bookcases and wooden benches, is where visitors are greeted, firewood is stacked, extra songbooks are stashed, and an ever-changing bulletin board follows the service work of our members around the world.

The second room opens off the first. It's a soaring space of tall windows, white walls, wainscoting, and rows of wooden benches that form a square around a woodstove nearly as old as the church. Kindling is neatly stacked in a woven basket beside the stove, while here and there a colorful afghan is thrown over a bench to warm one of our older members against the inevitable winter chill.

There is no furnace. No telephone. No cell service. No electricity.

Chuckling at our determined efforts to keep the world with its 24/7 electronics at bay, I open the car door and begin to unpack the miles of balsam and fir that my friend Dave has woven into garlands for our

blessed

Christmas celebration. I drag them through the snow to the church steps, drop them, then return to the car for candles, pinecones, and loose greens to lay on our windowsills, plus a dozen candles to line the snow-covered path from parking area to sanctuary.

A dozen or so families worship here each Sunday. But on Christmas night, more than a hundred men, women, and children come out of the hills and surrounding farms to fill the benches, sing carols, light candles, dream of miracles, and open their hearts to the Presence of God.

There will be the farmer from down in the valley who is trying to make sure there's a place for family farms in the 21st century. The legislator from a nearby village who wants to build a better community. The teen who left a difficult home and is taking the first tentative steps into a new life. The elderly woman embarked upon her last journey.

Afterwards everyone will gather around the huge Christmas fire in our woodstove to sip hot apple cider, munch on homemade cookies, greet neighbors, smile at strangers, talk about the weather, comment on the price of wood—and experience the strength and love of a faith community.

Hauling the last greens to the church, I plop down on the top step to catch my breath and think about the folks who will come to visit.

After the last log has tumbled into fiery sparks and the candles are low, they'll pull on parkas and mittens and, reluctantly, trudge out into the dark winter night. But before they reach their cars, they'll each pause and look back at the old church, the path to its door lit by a dozen glowing candles in the snow.

And, in some ancient way, each person will understand that no matter how dark the night or how difficult the path, the Light found here at this small church in the mountains will always overcome the darkness.

The Teapot

A silver teapot has been hung over a kitchen fire
for some seven generations of women.

As a winter storm roars through the woods and dumps several feet of snow in the firs surrounding my cottage, I reach up to pull down my great-grandmother Emily's silver teapot from the kitchen shelf on which it sits. Polishing silver is a lot better than shoveling snow in my book—and any day that's as cold as this one is a good day to catch up on stuff that never makes it to the top of my ongoing list of chores.

Carefully placing the teapot on my kitchen counter, I wondered, not for the first time, why the teapot was one of the trunkful of things my great-grandmother had chosen to bring to the United States when she left England a century ago. Nineteenth-century travel was tough, and I knew that she'd not only hauled the teapot across an ocean, she'd also dragged it three-quarters of the way across the United States. She and her husband had settled in New Mexico when it was a territory, then five or six children later they'd pulled up stakes and returned to England. Yet with all the complexity of moving a huge family by train, wagon, and ship, they'd still made room for the teapot.

Curious, I pushed the teapot closer to a light and studied it. The finish was badly tarnished. I hadn't been able to get to it—there were just too many other things that needed attention. Too many calls to return, bills to pay, kids to check on, and elderly aunts to visit. I sighed and began running hot water and lavender soap into the sink.

I didn't know much about my great-grandmother, I realized as I gently washed her teapot. I did know, however, that when her daughter Florence grew up, married, and immigrated to the United States with her husband and two tiny daughters, the teapot had gone along. The couple settled in Pennsylvania, and when their eldest daughter—also named Florence—grew up, married an army captain, and began a life that had her moving from one military base to another, she was given the teapot, too.

That Florence was my mother, which explains why I am standing in the kitchen up to my elbows in lavender suds, feeling guilty and looking at a tarnished, soapy pot.

I take the pot into my workroom and remove as much of the tarnish as possible. Thirty minutes later the old metal begins to glow with a rich, soft light.

Huh. I wonder how old it is? Thoughtfully, I turn the pot upside down and study the infinitesimally tiny marks on the bottom. Having seen one or two segments of the *Antiques Roadshow* as I surfed from one channel to another, I realize that these tiny marks are a clue. Quickly, I plunk the teapot on my worktable and reach for my laptop. Within minutes I am up to my eyeballs in British "hallmarks," as the tiny pictorial marks are called, and it's not long before I find what I'm looking for. The teapot was manufactured in Sheffield, England, by Morton & Company between 1742, when the process of melding sterling silver with a copper liner for teapots was developed, and 1785, when Morton & Company stopped registering hallmarks.

Yikes. I sat back in my chair and stared at the teapot. It was fully a hundred years older than I'd expected. And since the way it was made reflected silversmithing practices that had been used early on, the women in my family had apparently been polishing this teapot for more than 260 years.

Stretching back in my chair, I tried to envision what that meant. My family came from Sheffield. They had lived there when it was a small, rural metalworking village nestled among the Yorkshire hills. The techniques its metal workers developed in their homes had, along with those at various mills, given rise to both a British middle class and the Industrial Revolution. But anti-industrial violence in 1813 had ripped the village apart. Failed crops in 1816 had resulted in starvation. A cholera epidemic in 1832 had killed 402 people. A flood in 1857 had wiped out a third of the town's populace.

My great-grandfather, Emily's husband, had apparently had enough. He married Emily, packed the teapot, and headed for the United States somewhere, I suspect, in the 1870s. Now here I was, gently touching a teapot that had been hung over the kitchen fire by some seven generations of women in my family.

Holding the teapot in my hands, I can feel its strength and sturdiness. I can run my fingers over its dents, study the cracks in its bone lid ornament, lightly stroke the scorch mark on its side. Was it ever dropped on a kitchen hearth? Thrown across a room? Washed by one of my grandmothers' tears? Given the chaotic world through which it has traveled over the centuries, the answer's fairly obvious.

The thing is, it has survived. And I'm willing to bet that despite the fire, brimstone, and bullets that circle our planet today, this glowing little teapot—and the women who travel with it—will survive into the future as well.

Gently, I place it back on my kitchen shelf.

Making a Difference

The impulse to serve is the mysterious ingredient
that fills us up, that makes our cup run over.

—Robert Lawrence Smith, former headmaster of
Sidwell Friends School, in *A Quaker Book of Wisdom*

A Philadelphia Wedding

A woman's wedding reveals who she is—
or who she wants to be.

The bride was stunning.

Walking into the two-story ballroom of a historic house on one of colonial Philadelphia's narrow cobbled streets, Spring Moore moved confidently through the room's quiet elegance and up the aisle between rows of family and friends. Her floor-length white gown shimmered with rainy-day light from the arched windows lining the room, and a whisper of veil, caught in a knot of dark red curls at the back of her head, drifted behind as she walked.

The impossibly tall and blond bridegroom—today a 28-year-old computer whiz, but not far from the tow-headed boy I'd known since he was able to leap tall buildings in a single bound—waited with an Episcopal priest at the front.

After the ceremony, amid hugs and tears, I caught sight of the groom's mom, my best friend for a zillion lifetimes, across the room. As usual, Debbie was stunning—tall, with bright coppery hair, a ready smile, and ocean-blue eyes that reflected decades of summer sailing. Moving through the crowd around her, I sneaked in a quick hug.

"You're a mother-in-law!" I crowed. "Is Spring as great as she seems?"

Debbie hugged me back. "Yep. She's got a big heart. Wait till you see your dinner!"

My *dinner?* Puzzled, I moved aside as the photographer herded the family together for a family portrait, then let my husband lead me downstairs to a small but elegant dining room. In what had been the house's formal reception rooms a century or two earlier, the dining room was filled with chairs and tables swathed in white linen, each with a centerpiece of ivory roses and a bevy of crystal and silver. Men and women in formal black and white were adding final touches, while others began opening champagne in the adjoining greenhouse.

Conversation flowed, the bride and groom arrived, and we sat down to a simple but sumptuous feast: clever skewers of cherry tomatoes and watermelon with fennel, exquisite balsamic glazed figs wrapped in bacon, a grilled chicken breast with cherry jus lie, pan-seared seitan, the tenderest roasted asparagus I have ever eaten, a wild rice with cherry pilaf, and a sparkling salad of mixed spring greens, spiced pecans, manchego, and basil vinaigrette followed by—what else?—a slice of wedding cake.

Who was the caterer?

Curious, I asked one of the waiters. Turns out the food was prepared by the catering arm of MANNA, a nonprofit organization started by the First Presbyterian Church of Philadelphia 16 years ago to provide meals to those living with HIV/AIDS—90 percent of whom lived in poverty. Today, supported by a small core of professionals, MANNA volunteers deliver over 600,000 meals a year to those who are ill and in need. The catering service is one of the ways the organization supports its work.

"The karma couldn't be beat," Spring told me later. "We felt that if we were going to be spending a significant amount of money on a wedding, that at least some part of it should be given back to the community. In the end, it wasn't a question of which caterer, but one of 'Why would we hire anyone else?'"

Why indeed?

I've always thought that a woman's wedding reflects who she is—or who she would like to be. So even though I don't know my best friend's daughter-in-law very well yet, I think I'd like to. Because if this wedding is any indication, then Spring Moore is intelligent, thoughtful, compassionate, and one of God's very special creatures: A woman who will live her life in ways that will nurture us all—particularly those who are helpless, hurting, and hungry.

And that's a blessing.

Girls Matter

In Afghanistan, all it takes to help girls is three cups of tea.

Watching the exuberant girls gathered in front of Mt. Abe, a rambling fifties-style high school in the small town of Bristol, Vermont, is a joy.

School is over for the day, and to their minds, the girls have been set free. They toss their hair, text their friends, compare jeans, pogo up and down in excitement, laugh, shriek, make plans to meet at that night's basketball game, swap homework, and surreptitiously keep track of what the boys in nearby groups are doing.

They're bright, they're strong, and these girls know their worth.

To the teenage boys who hang out 10 feet away, pushing and shoving one another to show off their ability to leap tall buildings in a single bound, they are enchantment.

To the parents in minivans and trucks who pull up to the school's entrance to transport them to a zillion after-school activities, they are God's gift to the earth and an exhausting source of daily challenges.

To the teachers who work with them, they are both a delight and an exasperation—largely dependent on whether or not, at least today, the girls lived up to their potential or tested the boundaries of adolescence.

Heading into the school for an afternoon swim, I contrast the picture of these strong, confident young women who can read, write, think, sing, dance, and send a hockey ball smashing into the goal with the televised pictures I had seen last night of girls who live in Afghanistan. They are just as lively and just as bright. But there the similarity ends.

blessed

Afghanistan is rough. As most of us have slowly realized, the country is governed at the local level by male tribal leaders who often wrap their decisions in an interpretation of religious law that denies women an education.

While the Taliban ruled, not one girl was enrolled in school, and the ramifications have been huge. Few Afghani girls can read, write, or think critically about the world around them. Instead, they are married off by age 17 and imprisoned if they run away from their husbands.

What's more, with few educated women, there are few women doctors. And with few women doctors, as a report from the United Nations Girls' Education Initiative makes clear, many if not most Afghan women are denied even basic gynecological and obstetric health care. The result: Afghanistan has the second highest maternal mortality rate in the world.

Sighing, I step into the high school and turn down the corridor that leads to the pool.

Change comes slowly to Afghanistan. Even though the Taliban no longer rule, most girls are still married in their teens, and parents won't let them out of their sight or attend school for fear they'll be harmed by the Taliban or its supporters. Incredibly, the Taliban is responsible for having bombed or otherwise destroyed over 500 schools in the country—most of them schools that educate girls. In 2008 alone, reports UNICEF, 283 schools were violently attacked, leaving 92 dead and 169 injured. In one infamous incident, Taliban supporters threw acid on the faces of three young schoolgirls and left them writhing in the dirt.

But sometimes it takes only one person to make a difference in even the most challenging situations. In this case, Greg Mortensen, an American nurse and mountain climber who founded the nonprofit Central Asia Institute, decided to see what he could do to help.

Greg had learned about the lack of education for girls in Afghanistan when he was in neighboring Pakistan to climb K2—the second highest mountain in the world. He had become sick and disoriented during the climb and had wandered off the trail he was following. Villagers found him wandering in the mountains, brought him to their village, and nursed him back to health—an experience Greg chronicled in his book *Three Cups of Tea*. With one cup of tea, he and the villagers were still strangers, said one of the village leaders. By the second cup, they had become friends. By the third, they were family.

As he healed, Greg noticed the village children sitting together drawing letters in the dirt with sticks. The village couldn't afford a teacher or a school, but the children were so starved for knowledge that they were teaching themselves to read.

Deeply moved, Greg came home, sold everything he owned, and began raising money to help them build a school. He provided the materials; they provided the land and sweat equity.

Discovering that the plight of Afghani kids was just as bad if not worse, he became determined to help them as well. To date, working with local communities, over 78 permanent schools have been built in Pakistan and Afghanistan, 48 temporary ones have been launched, hundreds of teachers have been trained, and nearly 30,000 children have gone to school—two-thirds of them girls. It's an amazing achievement. And the Taliban has left them alone.

Calling hello to a couple of the Mt. Abe girls as I head into the ladies' locker room, I wonder what these newly educated young Afghani girls will do with their lives. The Mt. Abe girls have circled the globe, volunteered in Africa, and started innovative community-based heating programs for poor people in Vermont. They are a blessing to our community.

Given the chance, what will the young women of Afghanistan do?

Gracie's Friend

A passionate defender of the poor, the displaced, the hungry, and the innocent takes on the challenges of a Ukrainian orphanage.

Sitting down at the well-worn wooden table in the back of Almost Home, a café and culinary shop located in what had been an old Vermont country store in Bristol, I was sipping a steaming mocha latte that my friend Elizabeth had placed in front of me. Several town residents had wandered in to read the local papers, comment on town news, predict the weather, wait for a bagel, argue a little politics, and decry the banishment of Gracie, the store cat, from the premises.

"Can you believe it?" asked one tall woman who sat down at the table and launched a passionate defense of Gracie and an equally passionate attack on the low-life who had complained about the cat's presence.

I joined in on the denunciation—after all, Gracie was a sweetheart who greeted every visitor with great affection. But it wasn't long before I became intrigued with Gracie's defender, a woman I'll call Jan since she doesn't want to take credit for her good deeds.

Jan is a former Peace Corps volunteer who has been a passionate defender of the poor, the displaced, the hungry, and the innocent for more than 20 years. After her four children graduated from college and she could, finally, ease out of the single-working-mother-who-did-it-all lifestyle, at the age of 50 she'd volunteered for the Peace Corps.

"I was sent to Ukraine," Jan says with a shake of her head. "I was an accountant and one of the first Peace Corps volunteers sent in after the breakup of the former Soviet Union."

Not only was she one of the first, she was also part of a special group of American business volunteers who were sent to bring a variety of administrative skills and financial know-how to the newly independent country. Unfortunately, the city government that she was assigned to help couldn't quite figure out what to do with her. As a result, Jan spent a good amount of time wandering around the country getting to know local Ukrainians and learning about their lives.

When she returned to the States and began to think about what she might do next, she read a newspaper article about some Americans who were trying to help get kids off the streets in Kyiv, an ancient city in eastern Ukraine.

Jan knew about the street kids from her time abroad, but the problem had gotten worse. The kids were part of Ukraine's 100,000 or so "social orphans," an academic term that cloaks the reality that the children's parents are alive but have abused or abandoned them. The Ukrainian government puts these kids in orphanages, then dumps them, with few or no skills, on the streets at age 16. According to various organizations involved in the area, the Mafia sweeps in and offers them money. The results are predictable. Roughly 70 percent of the boys turn to a life of crime, 60 percent of the girls become prostitutes, and 10 percent of all kids coming from the orphanages commit suicide by age 17.

Reading the article, Jan knew she had to help. "I knew I couldn't get kids off the street," she says, "but I wondered if there was something I could do to keep them from getting on the streets to begin with."

The Vermont woman returned to Ukraine and hit the ground running. Apparently, the orphans most at risk were those with fetal alcohol syndrome, a label used to identify kids whose brains had been damaged in utero because their mothers consumed alcohol. Jan heard about one orphanage that housed these children from a Peace Corps volunteer who was leaving the country. Situated far from media attention in the Carpathian Mountains of western Ukraine, the Mykolychin orphanage was in desperate straights. Every time it rained, raw sewage backed up into the orphanage, flooding the dining room and children's shower area. It also washed away dirt in the orphanage's backyard—uncovering the garbage that the orphanage had been forced to bury there over the years.

"The first time I saw it, there was broken glass sparkling just everywhere," Jan says.

A new director had just been appointed, and Jan asked him why the garbage was being buried. She found that the city wouldn't pick up the orphanage's garbage unless they had a Dumpster. Horrified, she went out and bought two.

Then Jan began meeting with the new director to assess what else the kids needed. Many things—like bulldozing the orphanage's backyard and removing the garbage, glass, and contaminated soil—will take time. Other things—climbing walls for physically challenged children, eye surgery for a special child, new windows, and a new roof—have been done. And the city has agreed to replace the septic system next year.

But now that some of the more pressing needs have been addressed, Jan is focusing on helping the 14- and 15-year-olds, many of whom are mentally challenged, attain job skills that will allow them to support themselves when the state dumps them on the street in a year or two.

The new director has suggested that any training related to handwork will help. So Jan has formed the nonprofit organization UkraineWorks, Ltd., and is finding ways to raise funds for three sewing machines, knitting wool, woodcarving and woodworking tools, a loom for weaving rag rugs, and three or four computers.

It's an uphill battle, particularly given the economic uncertainty in the United States that's making all of us hang onto our wallets. But looking at Gracie's fierce defender sipping her coffee at Almost Home, I suspect that the kids at the Mykolychin orphanage will shortly be weaving, knitting, carving, and keyboarding themselves into a new life.

I Love Frankie

Escalating home foreclosures have doubled the numbers of
abandoned dogs and cats on the streets.

Looking down at my son's shaggy Portuguese/water/something-or-other dog, it was hard not to smile. I had slipped on my shoes and picked up his leash to go for a late afternoon walk. It was spring—and neither of us could get enough of the sweet spring flowers emerging along the street.

Most dogs would simply have pricked up their ears and trotted expectantly to the door.

Not Frankie.

Overflowing with a burst of joyous ecstasy his body couldn't contain, he had skidded over the wood floor in a series of fast spins—careening into a coffee table, knocking over a candle, and putting my son's low credenza of expensive electronics in jeopardy. Then, like a batter headed for home plate, he slid into a quivering sit at my feet.

I stayed quiet, facing the apartment door, leash in hand, and looked deeply into his intense brown eyes as he worked to calm himself.

Frankie was a rescue dog. He had been found skinny, dirty, and frightened in a part of Los Angeles with block after block of empty houses and litter-strewn gas stations. Dogs without Borders, a local non-profit group that works to find homes for abandoned dogs, had taken him in and placed him in foster care with my son Matthew.

It was a good arrangement. Matthew agreed to care for the dog, give him a refresher course in proper doggie behavior, and bring him to an adoption fair once a week so prospective families could check the dog out. In exchange, Matthew got free dog food and vet care—plus hours of exercise, a deep understanding of the intricacies of doggie biobags, and a devoted companion who lived only for the opportunity to gaze worshipfully at him from across the room.

For a young dog-loving screenwriter living in an isolating city and working in a chaotic industry, it was perfect. For a young dog who had been abandoned, terrorized, and left for dead, it was a gift from Heaven.

"Good boy, Frankie," I praised the dog at my feet. With all four feet thumping the floor as they tried to get away from him, he managed to stay in a sit and keep his eyes on mine.

"Good dog," I repeated as I dropped a chain collar with attached leash over his head. "Want to check out the flowers?"

Frankie is fortunate. Matthew adopted him permanently last year, and the mutt is now spoiled rotten by our entire family.

But other dogs have not been as fortunate. Across the United States, animal shelters report that since the wave of home foreclosures began a couple of years ago, the numbers of abandoned dogs and cats left locked inside foreclosed homes or running the streets have doubled. It's a tragedy that measures the desperation of families struggling to stay afloat—and it challenges those of us who are at least treading water to lend a hand.

Fortunately, incredibly wonderful people like Matthew have stepped forward. They've volunteered at local shelters to walk or foster abandoned dogs until permanent homes can be found. They've asked grocery stores to put bins at the fronts of their stores for donations of dog and cat food intended for shelters. They've cleaned out their basements and held garage sales to raise money for adoption organizations.

Their compassion and commitment is a blessing—and a lesson—for us all.

The Heart and Soul of Dorothy Selebwa

Think there's nothing one woman can do about a country of orphans?
Think again.

Driving along a two-lane road not far from Maine's rocky coast, the slow, heavy thrumming of crickets in a nearby meadow drifts in through the car window. Wild grasses and buttercups line the road's sandy shoulders, and far above, on a current of warm sea air, a broad-winged hawk glides across the sky.

Noting the black mailbox that's almost buried in wildflowers at the edge of the road, I turn into a short sandy drive that leads to a small house on the edge of a meadow. A gray-and-white cat sprawls in the sun, and as I enter the house through the open door, an elderly dog struggles to his feet to welcome me.

"Ellen, is that you?" calls a voice from somewhere within the house.

The dog peers sweetly up at my face and leans his head against my thigh for a pat. "Yup. I made it," I call back.

Two women emerge from another room and welcome me with warm smiles. We have never met before, but over the past few years, we have e-mailed a time or two about our mutual concern for the 3 million children who have been orphaned by AIDS in Kenya.

Suki Rice, a Maine woman who owns the house in which we meet, is tiny, with long gray hair, a quick giving manner, and swirling skirts. Dorothy Selebwa, who has come from Kenya to visit, is a tall woman with curly brown hair, dark chocolate eyes, a direct manner, and a solid faith that reaches into the heart of anyone who gets within 10 feet.

"El-len," she says in soft Kenyan accents as we hug. "It is so *good* to meet you."

The love I sense in this woman's heart is humbling. While most of us wring our hands in despair over the plight of 7 million children orphaned by Africa's AIDS epidemic, this woman—mother of 7, grandmother of 15, head of her church's regional committee on widows and orphans—has rolled up her sleeves, waded into a problem that has so far defeated 193 nations around the world, and done something to help the 3 million orphans in her home country of Kenya.

As we sit together in Suki's living room, Dorothy explains that her work began one hot day in 2001 when she and a committee of women were meeting at their church to discuss the care of widows and orphans in the Kakamega district. Generally they would talk about getting some clothing together and maybe a small monetary donation. But while they were meeting, two hungry children appeared at the door. "You can't refuse food to anyone when you have some," says Dorothy, and so the women shared their lunch. But at their next meeting, three children showed up. At the next, 10…then 20.

Of course, women were curious to know where the kids were coming from and why they were hungry. "We found out that their parents had died of AIDS," Dorothy says. "Some were roaming the countryside. Some had been taken in by aunties and uncles, but they didn't have the food to feed them. Most were living in grass shelters." When the rains came, the children got drenched. "They had not even a blanket," Dorothy says.

The government, preoccupied with other issues, would not help.

"So I said to the committee, 'Fine. We are the mothers. We bring children into this world. We will find a way to feed them,'" says Dorothy.

The church had no cooking facilities, so the women began cooking outside on stones and feeding the children under a tree. The numbers grew and stretched the committee's resources to the breaking point.

A year later, an American woman visiting the area invited Dorothy to the United States to share her work with an international group of churchwomen. Dorothy went, the group agreed to help with a small grant, and Suki Rice, the Maine woman in whose house we were meeting, volunteered to help Dorothy raise more money.

Suki places a cup of tea beside me as Dorothy tells what happened. Working together, church members of the Kakamega district and four Maine women who formed the nonprofit group Friends of Kakamega raised enough money for the Kakamega churchwomen to build a simple kitchen and dining hall. A year later, they were able to top it with 10 rooms to house at least some of the children. A year after that, they built a third floor with another 10 rooms. Then they bought 5 acres of surrounding land where they now raise vegetables and chickens to feed the kids.

Today the Kakamega Orphans Care Center houses 42 boys and girls, feeds a hot lunch to another 59 kids every day, and supports an additional 70 kids who live in the community with a relative. Community members, who make an average of $4 to $6 a month, leave a bag of beans or a bushel of corn at the care center as they are able.

There are two problems. One is that as AIDS slashes its way through the African continent, there are more homeless orphans wandering the countryside every day. The other is that, although boys and girls are housed on separate, supervised floors of the dormitory, the government—yes, the same one that can't seem to help the kids itself—told Dorothy in June that it will close the care center unless a separate structure is built to house the boys. And they'll close it by December of this year. It's a desperate but misguided attempt to stop the spread of AIDS.

Dorothy looks at me with quiet eyes. There's not much time. "We don't know whether to send the boys away or try to raise money for a new structure," she says simply.

By December it will be one or the other.

The Cookbook

Some cookbooks offer a blueprint for good food.
This one opens hearts.

Swinging off the dusty dirt road that leads down past the old Jerusalem Schoolhouse, I tuck the Prius in between two other cars, pick up a bag full of notebooks and pens, and head toward the schoolhouse steps.

Pink geraniums tumble out of window boxes, and my friends Blair and Linda have left the door propped open to the summer breezes skimming across the mountain and through the meadows.

Surrounded by wildflowers, a country store, a trailer where the guy who runs the snowplow lives, and, across the road, some of the school's early attenders now buried in a family plot, this simple one-room schoolhouse has become a place for neighbors to gather and celebrate everything imaginable.

"Hi, there!" I greet Blair and Linda as I dump my supplies on a table.

As we laugh and talk, I look around the well-used room and remember all the gatherings that have taken place here. Hefty 5:00 A.M. breakfasts are held for hunters in the fall, community carol sings cause an overflow at Christmas, an Easter pie sale in the spring triggers a traffic backup halfway to the state highway, and summer flea markets and picnics draw everyone but the bears out of the surrounding hills. And as if that's not enough, every other Sunday, the Reverend Molly Bidwell, an Episcopal priest and violinist who lives down the road, clears away some of the old chalk dust and offers bread and wine to the faithful.

For a 136-year-old clapboard building with a tin roof, questionable plumbing, and a fire truck tucked under one wing, the school redefines the notion of what a community center should be.

My friends Blair and Linda know this. Blair came to Mad River Glen to ski, married a man she met on the slopes, opened a B&B, and decided to stay forever. That was 45 years ago. Linda came a little later. She's only been here for 33 years—just long enough to raise some children, teach a few kids, and settle in.

Today both women are integral members of the community. They understand the necessity of a simple space in which neighbors can share a glass of lemonade, swap hunting stories, elaborate on the intricacies of the perfect woodpile, complain about the instability of satellite connections, and celebrate the goodness of living in a beautiful place with one foot in the past and the other in the future.

And that's why they agreed to help raise money for the school's restoration by pulling together a community cookbook. "There was a cookbook when I first came here some 30 years ago," says Linda. "It was a wonderful way to connect with Vermont cooking, and a wonderful way to connect with the community. So when Blair asked if I'd work on *this* cookbook, I agreed."

The cookbook was a huge undertaking. Sylvia Purinton's raisin bread, Heather Barnard's maple salmon, Cheryl Estey's jubilee jumbles, Reva Cousino's cucumber pickles, Linda's own fresh basil soup—all the dishes that show up at church potlucks, community picnics, fire company barbecues, and the dining-room table for Sunday dinner.

But when it was done, the cookbook sold out. At $12 a pop, and with printing costs essentially underwritten by ads from businesses in nearby communities, the *Jerusalem Schoolhouse Cookbook* put a nice chunk of change into the school's restoration fund.

And, as Linda and Blair had intended, the cookbook made the connections they had been hoping for among neighbors. Teachers, farmers, housewives, artists, small-business people, state legislators, loggers, a nurse—"It really connected the community," says a jubilant Linda. "I'd meet someone somewhere, recognize their name from the cookbook, and say, 'Oh! You wrote the ___ recipe!' Then we'd be off and talking about it."

Blair chuckles. "Or somebody would be making one of the recipes for dinner and they'd run into a problem. So they'd pick up the phone and call the person who wrote it. Then they'd talk about it"—and about everything else from property taxes and wind towers to coyotes and the best place to pick blackberries.

Sitting next to Blair and Linda in the schoolhouse, as old pull-down shades flutter in the soft summer breeze, I think about all the voices that have echoed through this room over time.

Like many communities, Jerusalem is in transition. Many of the "Old Vermonters" have largely owned the land and worked with their hands for generations. They know what it takes to struggle through a dark winter night at 20 below to search for a stray calf, boil sap 24 hours a day for two weeks straight, build their own homes, till the thin mountain soil, launch a small business, and, if need be, live on last year's apples from the cellar.

The "New Vermonters" are largely professionals or entrepreneurs who have come "from away" to start up small businesses from scratch or work from home—electronically connected to businesses flung around the world. They know what it takes to rip up their roots, empty their bank accounts, and risk every dime they'll ever make to move to a new place with no family and friends to support them when the going gets tough or times are lean.

The two groups are different. And sometimes that difference leads one person to misinterpret another's intention, or his words, and rail about the folks "from away" or the folks "who have been here forever."

But not here. Not at the Jerusalem Schoolhouse, where a community gathers to talk about its woodpiles, celebrate its maple syrup, complain about its satellite connections, and nibble on dish after dish of good Vermont cooking.

Not here, where a cookbook can open hearts.

The K9 Connection

Match a homeless shelter dog with an at-risk teen and what
do you get? A new chance for both.

Sprawled under a market umbrella in the piazza outside Starbucks in
the California coastal town of Marina del Rey, Pinky, a 40-pound pink
American Pit Bull Terrier, was unaware of all the attention she was
attracting.

Instead, she was focused on the biscotti crumbs that had fallen on
my sneaker. I chuckled as the huge muzzle wuffled my toes and the
brain inside an equally huge head tried to figure out what was foot and
what was crumb.

This? Yes.

This? Yes.

This? Oops. Maybe not. Mortified, she stopped nuzzling my shoe-
lace and looked at it more carefully. It was an important lesson, and I
didn't rush her. Sneakers are expensive.

An older guy sitting at a nearby table watched for a moment, sipped
his latte, then leaned forward to ask my son about the dog.

"That's a pit bull, isn't it?"

My son, a 29-year-old screenwriter who lives in the neighborhood,
smiled. "Sure is."

The guy nodded. "I thought so." He flashed Pinky an admiring
glance. "The pink glitter-collar kind of threw me off."

As my son began to talk about Pinky and her special place in the community, I thought about the collar. A lot of us think that pit bulls eat people for breakfast. But Pinky didn't get the memo. And for all her size and strength, a pink glitter-collar is an accurate reflection of who she is. Pinky is sweet. She's gentle. She's loving. She's steady as a rock. And, as a member of the K9 Connection, a Santa Monica–based program that matches homeless shelter dogs with at-risk teens, she's also one of the best teachers on the planet.

The K-9 Connection is a special organization, funded and supported by a variety of resources, including the Santa Monica Police Department, Fox Studios, Creative Artists Agency, "Dog Whisperer" Cesar Millan, and film directors Martin Scorsese and Tony Scott. Founded two years ago as an offshoot of a Santa Monica community center, the nonprofit group runs three-week sessions in which kids who have behavior issues or a history of running away, substance abuse, fighting, or gang activity are each assigned a shelter dog. The dogs, mostly mutts like Pinky who have been lost, abandoned, or abused, usually need to learn social and obedience skills before they can be put up for adoption.

The kids learn how to train the dogs to control impulsive and inappropriate behavior with positive reinforcements—a lesson that will serve both dogs and kids as each works to build a new life.

The bond between child and dog is strong, and for kids who have been in trouble, it's sometimes the only connection they've been able to make in a long time. The hope among program volunteers like my son is that the kids will use that connection as a bridge to the rest of us.

Time will tell. In the meantime, Pinky is nuzzling biscotti here in the piazza. Having graduated from the K9 program and having taught her kids a gentler way of life, she's waiting for someone to take her home.

Jambo!

When Kenyan orphans needed help, women—from Africa to the
United States and Canada—held potluck suppers, bake sales, raffles,
and did whatever else it took to raise money for the kids.

Singing, clapping, dancing, and cheering, a procession of middle-school
boys and girls in brightly colored shirts, shorts, dresses, and skirts wound
their way through the narrow, dirt-packed lanes of Kakamega, their red
flip-flop sandals happily slapping the red Kenyan dirt.

It was moving day for the boys. A new dorm had just been completed
about 6 minutes down the road from the Kakamega Orphans Care
Center, where the children lived—and the girls were giving the boys a
cheering escort as they moved into the new shelter.

Here and there, eager hands supported a dozen or more wildly pat-
terned mattresses over their heads, and laughter made quick work of a
task that—just one year ago this month—had seemed impossible.

That was when the Kenyan government, in a misguided attempt
to halt the spread of AIDS, had told the Care Center's founder, Dorothy Selewba, that she'd have to have separate dorms for boys and girls
within four months—or else the government would close down the
Care Center and turn its residents back out onto the streets from which
most had come.

Horrified, Dorothy turned to her church community for help.
The 42 children, all of whom had been orphaned by AIDS, had managed to help the Care Center become partly self-sufficient by planting

5 acres with maize and sweet potatoes. They'd learned how to use sewing machines, raise chickens, prepare meals, wash clothes by hand—all while attending school full-time.

But a dorm? How were children supposed to raise a building?

Word spread from Africa to the United States and Canada, and women of all faiths on both continents came forward to hold potluck suppers, bake sales, raffles and whatever else it took to raise money for the children.

Front and center were the women of *Curves*, the fitness centers founded by Diane Heavin and her husband. Once *Curves'* members learned about the children's plight, they pulled together and contributed nearly *half* of the $40,000 cost of a new dorm and the land on which to build it. One woman, who had tragically just lost her son, asked friends to contribute to the Care Center's children in his name—then contributed a major portion of her son's life insurance policy to the effort as well.

A joyful Dorothy expressed her gratitude over and over. Then the intrepid Kenyan rolled up her sleeves, bought the land, and got the project under way.

But just as *Curves* cofounder Diane Heavin was packing for a trip to visit the children, violence erupted in Kenya. Disagreements between two presidential candidates led to rioting between their tribes that spread to even remote areas like Kakamega. People were beaten and killed. Stores were burned or closed, cars overturned and torched. Homes were burned, food became impossible to find, and gasoline disappeared.

Fortunately, the Care Center had been closed for the Christmas holiday, and the children—each with huge bags of food, cooking oil, and soap—had been sent to visit their legal guardians in remote villages.

Although communication was dangerous, Dorothy made sure the children knew to stay put. When the worst of the danger finally passed—largely due to the intervention of former UN secretary Kofi Anann, who arbitrated a settlement between the warring candidates and their tribes—the children returned, and construction on the dorm was completed.

Today, the placid pace that characterizes Kenyan life has resumed at least on the surface. But thousands of residents remain in "displaced persons camps" throughout Kenya, and the children's Care Center itself has swelled to support 150 kids. Some are housed in the dorms, others are housed with members of the community and fed at the center.

Food and gasoline costs have doubled, as has the cost of seed and fertilizer. Nevertheless, the Care Center's children are learning how to garden organically, and their 5-acre farm has been planted with vegetables, maize, and luceana trees—a local tree that feeds the soil with nitrogen, makes fodder for the cows, and can be harvested for firewood in one year.

Today, the people of Kenya have dropped from the headlines, but they are still deeply troubled. Displaced-persons camps remain, burned-out homes scar the landscape, violence unpredictably erupts, and the old and the young suffer a heavy toll from food shortages.

Scars from the past nine months will take decades to heal. Nevertheless, the 150 children now supported by the Care Center have been saved. They are housed, clothed, fed, and go to school. And they know that somehow, somewhere in the world, there's a whole community of women who love them.

A Christmas Blessing

Tonight, no one will go hungry.

In the gathering dusk, men and women in dark parkas and shaggy wool caps slowly begin to emerge from the neighborhood's side streets and move haltingly down Winooski Avenue.

Heads down, hands shoved in pockets against the cold, they silently pass windows lit for the holidays and move toward a huge warehouse.

The warehouse is located 10 or 11 blocks north of the Victorian homes and upscale shops for which the city of Burlington, Vermont, has, time and again, been rated "one of the 10 best places to live in America" by a slew of national media. But here there are no houses trimmed in lacy gingerbread and no chic shops. Instead, sagging homes line the street surrounding the warehouse, which—along with a small kitchen—is home to the Chittenden County Emergency Food Shelf.

"Hi, how are you doing?" I ask as I open the door. A freezing rain pelts the 60 or so men and women gathering outside the building as I slip inside. There, despite an out-of-order oven, eight volunteer students from the University of Vermont (UVM) are working furiously to bake chicken, warm up TaterTots, reheat donated pizza, chop vegetables, make peanut butter and jelly sandwiches, and put bananas and beverages within easy reach of anyone who comes through the door.

Dressed in hooded sweatshirts, jeans, and khakis, the group is young, enthusiastic, and dedicated. With $85 from UVM, they shop for food bargains at PriceChopper every Sunday afternoon; scavenge for pizza seconds at American Flatbread, Uno's and Domino's; sweep up not-quite-stale pastries at Starbuck's; swing by Klinger's bakery for leftover bread; and arrive here at the food shelf by 4:30 P.M.

Six nights a week, the Salvation Army makes dinner for those who have fallen through the safety nets of city, state, and nation. But on Sunday, the Army's day of rest, the UVM kids take over and make sure that anyone who's hungry gets fed.

This year the program is headed by a tall, blond chemistry major from Ohio who is all heart and organization. At age 22, senior Carly Hodgins has been a part of this group for four years and knows what she's doing. At 4:40 P.M, she bursts through the door loaded with bags of bread, boxes of pizza, a car full of kids, and within minutes every hand is scrubbed, chicken is in the oven, salad is being tossed, pizza is warming on the stovetop, and I am chopping what seem to be a zillion carrots.

As I work, I listen to the kids. They're focused on the men and women who will come through the door in less than an hour, and they clearly understand the issues surrounding hunger. While 96,000,000,000 pounds of food are thrown away every year by the food industry—that's *96 billion* pounds—someone in 1 out of every 10 households in the United States is either hungry today or at risk of being so tomorrow.

Why they are is a matter for sociologists and politicians to debate. But for these kids, the matter is simple: When somebody's hungry, you feed him.

"Time to open up!" Carly yells.

The door swings open. Men and women who've been waiting outside silently flow into the building, single file. There's no pushing or shoving. Just focused intent. Ten steps inside the door, each man or woman picks up a waiting plate, and the kids start piling it with food. Each person gets a single portion of meat, vegetables, salad, potatoes, and pizza. When the last person heads for a table, those who've been through the line can come back for seconds. The kids will serve until they run out of food.

Carly stands at the end of the food line and offers a beverage. "Apple juice?" she asks, looking straight into the eyes of each diner. "Orange juice?" Her smile is a flash of sunshine, her warmth a benediction.

As she reaches out to steady someone's hand, I remember words buried long ago in my heart: *"I was hungry and you gave me food. I was thirsty and you gave me something to drink. I was a stranger and you welcomed me."*

When the last meal has been served and the last diner has gone back into the darkness, I wipe down a steel table in the kitchen and think about what these kids have accomplished: Tonight, no one in Burlington will go hungry.

Village 2 Village

In one window, a manager. In another, a menorah. And an electric Santa waves from a window down the street. In neighborhoods all across America, families throw themselves into a variety of traditions that define faith, nurture belief, and give meaning to their lives.

Christmas eve is huge at the Kroll house on East Street. Tucked away on a quiet block in the village of Bristol, Vermont, the house overflows with the exuberant activities of four of Laurie and Michael Kroll's five kids as they get ready for church.

There's Christi, their beloved 19-year-old, who is studying to become a teacher at Taylor University in Indiana. There's her equally adored twin Danielle, who is taking a year off from school to work for a contractor. Then there are Jonathan and Joshua, the 11-year-old boys the Krolls adopted when the kids were 4 months old. More than likely one is still focused on his French horn, while the other is running up and down stairs looking for misplaced socks, shoes, or tie.

"I used to prepare a meal for everyone on Christmas Eve," says Laurie. "But church is at 7:00 P.M. and it was just too crazy around here." She shakes her head helplessly and laughs. "Now I just put out some appetizers."

The appetizers are a family tradition. But missing from the pre-Christmas festivity is the Kroll's 29-year-old adopted son James, who heads an orphan-care center Laurie founded in Uganda called village2village. Also missing is Michael Kroll—the Reverend Michael Kroll, that is—who's likely already at the First Baptist Church getting ready for the Christmas Eve service.

The tall, stately church itself, nearly 200 years old, glows with light across a narrow street from the village green. It's already draped with pine boughs and garlands, with candles standing on either side of the gleaming pulpit, and huge wreaths—handmade by church members—hanging on the church's equally huge double mahogany doors to symbolize the unbroken circle of God's love. The sidewalk in front of the church has been whisked clear of snow, and Christmas lights draped over the band shell on the village green glow softly through the trees.

Everything is ready.

All across America, December is the month in which we enthusiastically throw ourselves into a wide variety of traditions that define our faith, nurture our beliefs, and give meaning to our lives.

Nearly 180 million Christians celebrate the birth of Jesus on December 25, while 6 million Jews celebrate Hanukkah, the Festival of Lights, at around the same time of year. In addition, many of the 6 million American Muslims celebrate the Muslim New Year—Al-Hijra/Muharram. And scattered between and among all these celebrations are the people who cherish the season's good feelings, sit on Santa's lap, and look for an opportunity to celebrate family and give of themselves.

For Christians like Laurie, Christmas is both a celebration of the birth of Jesus Christ and a time in which to practice the selfless giving that became the hallmark of Jesus's life and teachings.

Laurie and Michael Kroll take that to heart. For them, Christmas actually starts four weeks before Christmas Day, when they light the first candle on their advent wreath—a small wreath placed in the center of a table with four purple or pink candles on the rim and a tall white pillar candle in the center.

Traditionally, that first candle, representing hope in the world, is lit each night before Christmas as prayers are prayed and Scripture read, says Laurie. A second, third, and fourth candle representing peace, joy, and love are lit in subsequent weeks. On Christmas Day itself, the tall white candle in the wreath's center, which represents Jesus, is finally lit, and the circle glows.

Once the first candle has been lit, the Krolls happily flow into holiday mode with church craft bazaars, silver teas, cookie exchanges, and chopping down the perfect Christmas tree.

In many ways, it's a traditional American Christmas. What makes it particularly meaningful, however, is the December church meeting that focuses on 60 orphans served by the village2village project in Serere, Uganda.

Laurie, a former social worker, launched the village2village project several years ago when a local camp counselor from Uganda visited and described how the children in his country were being victimized by violence and AIDS. Now, more than 1.4 million Ugandan adults who were HIV positive have died from AIDS alone—leaving behind 1.8 million children without access to health care, an education, or social services. By next year, Laurie says, that total is expected to reach 2.1 million children.

When the members of Laurie's church heard about the situation, they formed a group to look at how they could help. Now, every December, James Mutaka Kroll, the Kroll's adopted Ugandan son who runs the project in Serere, gives Laurie a list of what the kids need most, and the group turns itself inside out to meet at least a small percentage of the kids' needs.

That tradition of giving is one of the things that gives special meaning to the Christmas Eve service at First Baptist, says Laurie. When Michael Kroll steps down from his pulpit to light the Christmas candles as his congregants sing *Silent Night, Holy Night,* every one of those gathered in the sanctuary understands that the miracle of the Christmas they celebrate is centered in their hearts—and in a small village of children 7,000 miles away.

One Day, One Thousand Dresses

When two Vermont moms decide it's time to move beyond the backyard fence, even international borders can't hold them back.

As the first light of another frigid Vermont morning touched the town hall clock in Bristol, cars began to pull into parking spaces around the town green, doors slammed, and a trickle of what would eventually turn out to be 180 women began to carefully make their way down icy sidewalks and into the hall.

Navigating around tables already loaded with fabric, scissors, sewing machines, thread, and glue, they called greetings to one another, chucked their parkas onto a bench, stepped over power cords, grabbed a cup of hot coffee from the nearby pot, then began to snip, stitch, laugh, iron, tease, and trade stories about kids, dogs, in-laws, and next year's garden.

They sounded like women everywhere. But when they were done 12 hours later, stacked around them were 1,000 T-shirt dresses that, courtesy of a local cosmetics research company, would soon be on their way to needy widows and children orphaned by AIDS in Lusaka, the capital of Zambia.

"I got involved initially because of my neighbor Darla," says 49-year-old Nancy Luke, mother of two, proprietor of a custom drapery business in the village and head of the local chapter of Mothers without Borders, which sponsored the event.

Kids are Nancy and Darla's passion, and for years the two women have been involved in local church and school activities that focused on children. They hadn't done anything on a global level, but when they heard about the 800,000 Zambian children who had been orphaned by AIDS, plus the untold numbers of poverty-stricken widows roaming the Zambian countryside—"Darla heard it on Oprah or something"—they decided it was time to act. "Our kids had gotten big enough not to need constant supervision," Nancy says, "so we were able to look out a bit beyond the backyard fence."

The women heard about Mothers without Borders, checked it out, and liked what they saw. The organization had been started by a woman who first began helping children as the result of a church mission trip to Romania. Ninety-four percent of the money it raised went directly to services for women and children.

Today the organization has projects in several countries including Zambia, which is one of the poorest countries on the planet. Nearly 17 percent of the country's 11 million adults are infected with HIV, and a study from the Zambia Ministry of Health reports that 25 percent of pregnant women in urban areas like Lusaka are HIV positive. For those children who manage not to become infected at birth from their HIV positive mothers, the average life expectancy is 42 years.

Once they heard that, Nancy and Darla got busy. They sent out e-mails to friends, and distributed fliers to their neighbors, inviting them to a meeting. "About eight women showed up," Nancy says. "And—this is *so* typical of these women—they immediately picked a project and said, *'Let's do it! Let's do it now! Let's jump in over our heads!'*"

Nancy shakes her own head.

The first project the group tackled was assembling newborn kits. About 50 women showed up to help, and the kits were assembled, packed, and sent on their way. But for the second project, the Vermont women upped the ante. They put out collection boxes for sewing supplies at local hairdressers, parent/child centers, preschools, and a food co-op, then scheduled what has now become known as the first "sew-a-thon."

Most groups that get together to make T-shirt dresses make about 10, Nancy explains. "But when we heard how many were needed, we decided to make 1,000." So at Nancy and Darla's invitation, 180 women from the tiny village of Bristol and the surrounding countryside showed up to make 1,000 T-shirt dresses for Zambian women and girls. Autumn Harp, a local cosmetics research firm, picked up the tab for shipping.

Nor was that the end of it. Inspired by their success, Nancy and her Mothers without Borders group have scheduled a second sew-a-thon in just a few weeks. Yes, the temperature's close to zero.

Yes, there's snow in the forecast.

Yes, it's dark in the morning.

But with all the community support the group has received, Nancy suspects they'll make even more dresses than before.

"I think one of the reasons we're so successful is that, particularly during these hard times, some women can't give money, but they can give time," says Nancy. "They can give three hours, a piece of fabric, and themselves. And *that* can make a difference."

Eat, Pray, Knit

Two Connecticut women have given birth to a circle of women around the world who knit shawls that offer comfort, prayers, blessings, and warmth to thousands who are lost, bereaved, afraid, or in need.

Sitting beside the fire as the autumn temperature drops outside and my little French bulldog snores on the hearth, I reach into my yarn basket and gently pull out my latest project—a shawl for a friend who lives in the village.

The woman has had some serious challenges this year—the death of a dearly beloved grandmother, unexpected illness, unemployment, a chronically ill husband, the care of an adult with special needs. Between health challenges, money worries, and grief, she's had a lot on her plate. So I'm knitting her a shawl that will keep her warm, remind her she's surrounded by friends, and wrap her in our love.

Lavender and purple wool cascade through my fingers as I lift the half-finished shawl onto my lap, layering me in the soft wool from a local sheep farm in Middlebury. I stroke the yarn for a moment, almost able to smell the sweet grass of the sheep barn, then pick up my needles and begin to knit. *Knit 3, purl 3, knit 3, purl 3.* I get to the end of the row, turn, and reverse the pattern—*purl 3, knit 3, purl 3, knit 3*—weaving good intentions and prayers into every stitch.

I got the idea of making what's called—depending on your spiritual tradition—a prayer shawl, tallis, hajib, or, simply, a peace shawl—from

Vicky Gallo, a Connecticut mom in her mid-forties who works for her local cable company.

How Vicky got the idea is a little more complicated. A little more than 10 years ago, she and another Connecticut woman, Janet Bristow, a mom and a special-needs tutor, were attending the Women's Leadership Institute at Hartford Seminary. "I was just looking to expand my spirituality as a woman." Vicky shrugs. "Traditionally, we think that we're made in the image of God. But what does that mean when you're a woman?"

Good question. "It opened a big door," says her friend Janet. But after a year's study and a lot of discussion and prayer, the two women felt they had a glimmer of the answer. And they were ready to follow where the Spirit led. But where was that?

Actually, Vicky had gotten a clue years before when she was pregnant. Her mother, a deeply spiritual woman, owned a shawl made by Vicky's husband's aunt that she took everywhere. One day while Vicky and her mom were on vacation with their families, Vicky ran into trouble. She was three months pregnant with her second son and on the verge of a miscarriage. "My mom gave me her shawl and told me to pray," says Vicky. "So I put the shawl over my abdomen and, surrounded by my entire family, I prayed."

Seven months later, she gave birth to a healthy boy who this year just started his freshman year in college.

The second clue, Janet says, came when one of their classmates at the Hartford Seminary wrapped herself in a brightly colored Mexican shawl and asked the class to pray over it for her husband, who was ill. All 50 women laid their hands on the shawl and on her and joined their prayers to hers. Moments later, the classmate left for the hospital to be with her husband.

The next time Janet and Vicky saw the shawl it was on the altar at his funeral service. Afterward, they saw their classmate, who had once again wrapped it around her body.

"That's when I got it," says Janet. The love and blessing conveyed by that shawl were a source of comfort. "Intuitively I knew what we were supposed to do."

The process of creating a prayer shawl is simple. In their book, *The Prayer Shawl Companion,* Janet and Vicky suggest you plan a shawl with the recipient in mind. What colors will lift them up? What textures will soothe? Then, when you're ready to knit, hold the yarn in your hands and recite a blessing, pray, or just sit quietly for a moment. As you work, pray or think about the person who will receive your shawl. Remember what it feels like to be held by someone who cares for you. Then, "Pray those memories into your knitting along with thoughts of strength, peace, and healing for the one who will receive the work of your hands."

Today, with 3,000 groups attached to local religious institutions alone, the Prayer Shawl Ministry has somewhere between 50,000 and 60,000 women knitting and praying—and that doesn't include the gazillion more who, like me, make the traditional casserole for a friend in need, then pick out some wool, pray, and start to knit.

"It's overwhelming," says Vicky, who is amazed by the response of women around the world. "There's the woman who makes sure that the families of every fallen soldier get a shawl when the soldier's body is returned to Dover Air Force Base." She has 256 groups that have made almost 4,000 shawls for those killed and wounded in action. "Then there's the Habitat for Humanity people in Venice, Florida, who not only build someone a house but also make a shawl and wrap them up with it in ecumenical blessings. And the group in Tennessee who sent me a video about their work that just made me cry.

"There are so many groups popping up all over the place that we don't even know how many there are. Knitting prayer shawls is huge in Canada, very large in England, and we hear quite a bit from Australia, South Africa, and South America.

"It's just huge," she repeats. "Janet and I both work full-time, then come home and answer e-mails every night. I cannot think of any other ministry in our day or our time that touches as many people of so many backgrounds and faiths. It's like weaving together a cloth of faith. It shows you can put people of all faiths together and they find common ground."

Turning Vicky's words over in my mind as I knit, I also remember the words written by Professor Miriam Therese Winter, Vicky and Janet's mentor at the Hartford Seminary, in the foreword to their book: *"As our world unravels bit by bit in various ways, countless circles of compassion are knitting it back together again, one stitch at a time."*

What an incredible blessing.

Swapping Fire for the Sun

When Californian Marie Pimental saw women in Nigeria forced to
endanger the babies strapped to their backs as they balanced huge
baskets of firewood on their shoulders, she headed off into the African
bush to teach women how to swap fire for the sun.

When I ask 77-year-old Marie Pimentel how on earth a Wisconsin farm
girl ended up teaching solar cooking to the women of Uganda, Zambia,
Zimbabwe, Mozambique, Nigeria, and Rwanda, her sweet laugh tum-
bles through the phone line.

"It's a calling from the Holy Spirit," she chuckles. "It's so clear.
Opportunities have opened to us that wouldn't have otherwise. And the
fact that we have the energy and health to do this at our age, well, our
doctors are amazed!"

The "we" of whom Marie speaks is she and her 81-year-old husband,
Wilfred, a retired veterinarian who could probably be held responsible
for putting both of them on the road some 37 years ago.

In 1969 he packed up the family and moved them to Nigeria so
he could teach veterinary medicine. But while they were there, the
Pimentels noticed three things: One, that there were few trees, no new
trees were being planted, and, as a result, the Sahara Desert was advanc-
ing; two, that the smoky cooking fires women traditionally used were
the equivalent of smoking 10 to 20 packs of cigarettes a day and responsible for so many respiratory and eye ailments according to experts; and

three, that women, who were traditionally responsible for cooking a hot meal every evening, were always scrounging for wood and carrying huge baskets of firewood for long distances on their shoulders.

The Pimentels were upset. Not only were the women becoming ill and depleting a vanishing natural resource, they were inadvertently endangering their infants. They carried the children tied to their backs, and, tragically, not infrequently one of those huge baskets of firewood would slip and decapitate a child.

Marie couldn't stand it. But neither of them could figure out what to do, so after Wilfred's work was finished, they went home to California and focused on raising their five children. Then, in 1988, Marie heard about an international organization on solar cooking being formed in Sacramento. It turns out that a couple of cardboard boxes, some black spray paint, a dab or two of glue, and a roll of aluminum foil can create a box that catches the sun's rays and uses them to cook food placed inside.

Remembering the decapitated children in Nigeria, Marie jumped on the idea. "It really intrigued us," says Marie. "We wondered how it could be applied to Africa."

Nigeria was unstable at the time, but by 1994 Marie and Wilfred were able to meet with people in Kenya and get Rotary International to take a look at their idea. The Rotary is a volunteer organization made up of business and professional people, and Marie and Wilfred met with the organization's clubs in Nairobi to see if they would like to get involved in the project. They asked members to help evaluate the Kenyans' needs of Kenyans, whether or not a solar cooker would meet those needs, and to figure out how people might best be trained to use the cooker. Eventually, the Pimentels found non-governmental church and community groups that could bring people together for training, then follow up to see how the cookers were actually working out.

Not that recruitment was easy. "You're taking women who have been building fires for most of their lives and telling them to use sunshine instead," says Marie. "Now that's asking for a leap of faith!"

Nevertheless, it's a leap the women of Kenya made—and, to date, the women of 11 other countries as well. Today, 12 years later and 35 years after she first became aware of the effects of wood-burning cooking fires on the Nigerian women and their children, 15,000 women now use solar cooking, and Marie Pimentel is still returning to Africa several times a year.

"After all these years, it's like going home," says Marie, who refuses to let the aches and pains of aging slow her down. "The people are wonderful. They're so poor, but they're so generous."

The trip is a little more arduous than it used to be, she admits. "We're up and running by 6 every morning, and by 8 or 8:30 at night we're ready to drop. But sometimes we have social obligations with people in the area. They're younger, and they don't realize that Wilfred, who's 81, likes to have a nap!"

She laughs delightedly. "Our faith has given us the strength we need," she says firmly. "There are just so many good people. And so much to do."

Reinventing Who You Are

*It's all about waking up. At some point, you wake up
and realize that your life is half over and brimming
with the things that are your responsibilities—
not the things that give it meaning.*

—Kathleen A. Brehony, Ph.D., in *Prevention* magazine's
"Mess Up Your Life!" (July 2002)

The Secret

Studies reveal that women over 50 are the happiest. Here's the secret.

"Why didn't you tell me?" I demanded.

My stepmother just laughed, tossed another card onto the discard pile between us, and shrugged her shoulders. "You wouldn't have believed me," she said simply.

I glanced around the cool white-on-white apartment in exasperation. Playing cards after dinner with Edna Thulin Watts down in Florida is always a learning experience. Whether the conversation travels over family, real estate, manners, health, high tides, biblical truth, or a sale at the local Walgreens, I usually hear something unexpected. And this time was no exception.

You wouldn't have believed me.

The truth of those words pushed past my annoyance and marched into my brain.

She was right. What woman in the midst of the crazy run-here-run-there life of a 40-something would ever have believed that life after perimenopause and the what-should-I-do-with-the-rest-of-my-life questions is richer, fuller, and happier than at any other time?

My stepmother tapped one well-manicured nail on the pickup pile in front of me. "Your turn, girl."

My turn indeed. Picking a card at random, my fingers kept the game going while I thought about my life after the crazy hormone swings of perimenopause. Studies from Harvard to Wisconsin report that life is much richer and more satisfying now than at any other life stage. Unfortunately, the studies weren't set up to tell me why. But thinking about my stepmother's life and thinking back on my own, I suspect that the sheer joy of life in my fifties rests on the fact that…

I've got guts. Once you've rescued small children from certain death and maybe walked along the edge of a knife yourself, nothing much intimidates you. Taking risks—quitting your job, tossing your retirement money into a new business, telling evil people to mend their ways—is not only easy, it's addictive. The sense of freedom and the rush of sheer joy are like nothing else on the planet.

I'm comfortable with my body. No matter how many extra pounds pad your hips or how far your breasts sag, this is the body that grew a child, gave it life, and nourished it until it could stand on its own two feet. Forget about cellulite. A body that has nourished a child is glorious.

Chocolate cravings disappear. If every diet you've ever started has been sabotaged the day before your period by a clawing craving for a chocolate Tastykake, now you can relax. If you decide to shave a few pounds from those padded hips, it's now totally doable.

I know what's important. Family. God. Compassion. Forgiveness. Honesty. Love. Extending a helping hand. Everything else is chopped liver.

Stress isn't as big a deal. It's been a constant for so many years that you've learned how to deal with it and put the stressors in perspective.

I know who I am. I'm bigger, bolder, and brighter than some people feel comfortable with, I hug just about anyone who comes within range, and I rescue dogs, cats, and little old ladies. I'm not the person I want to be, at least not yet, but I like who I am on the journey.

I've got money. Kind of. I may not be sitting on a pot of gold, but there are no more $100,000 per child educations to fund and I'm making more money than I ever dreamed possible at age 20.

My relationships are solid. All the interpersonal relationship things that caused upheavals throughout my life are pretty much settled. I've come to terms with the fact that, no, my mother did not love me as much as she should have, and, yes, my mother-in-law would probably have preferred to have her son all to herself. But the man I married worships the ground I walk on, our son adores every hair on my head, my friends think I'm the best thing since sliced bread, my colleagues respect me, and my neighbors feel that I make the best maple cream cake on three planets. Who can complain?

I'm tolerant. Small people doing small things are more likely to illicit a compassionate response than make me angry. I know they must be hurting inside.

I can eat cereal for dinner. And it doesn't have to be granola.

I can jump into the hot tub naked. Caution: If you try this yourself, keep in mind that high-flying aircraft can see more than you think.

I can grab my husband. And make mad, passionate love in the middle of the living-room floor in the middle of the day. I just have to remember to lock up the dogs.

I can let somebody else drive. Looking back, I can see God's fingerprints all over my life. A nudge here, a stop sign there, a barrier where I was about to run off the road—I didn't arrive on this page or in your hands by accident. And that knowledge allows me to stay centered even in the eye of a storm.

The Perfect Weight-Loss Motivator

A sudden injury can build strength.

Pain sucks.

As I haltingly start to cross the living room, pain rips through my knee, convulses my back, and locks onto my wrist. "Oh, great!" I mutter to Rufus, the concerned little Westie who's following closely behind my brand-new walker.

I stop and shake my hand to loosen it up. "Now my hand's gone numb!"

Fortunately, there's no one around but the dogs to hear my grumpy complaining. My husband has fled to the gym, and if he's smart, he'll stop by the market and take a long time choosing some cantaloupe.

I give up on trying to restore feeling in my hand, grasp the walker as best I can, transfer my weight off my injured knee, and step out once again. "O-o-oo…"

The unconscious moan adds its patina to the cacophony of misery with which I've surrounded myself. As an active woman with places to go and people to see, I am not handling this injury well. I have books to write, interviews to conduct, planes to catch, a house to run, pets to feed, a garden to plan, and a family that is used to lots of love, a practical mind, and a helping hand.

Today none of that is getting done. Instead, I lurch across the living room toward the kitchen with an increasingly concerned Westie in my wake. I turn to reassure him—and find that an equally concerned French Bulldog has fallen in behind.

Terrific. Now we're a conga line.

Collapsing into a chair by the kitchen counter, I allow myself the luxury of a small scream as my back spazzes and a sharp pain slices through my knee. Then I shake my numb hand again and reach for the coffee.

Looking out the window into the morning sunshine, I realize that I've gotten myself into this situation. I had decided to ramp up my swim workout to burn more calories and strengthen my back, which tends to be twingy. I did it carefully. I hired a physical therapist who was also a competitive swimmer, and the routine she came up with was a winner. Unfortunately, there's no way she could have predicted I'd lose focus for a moment and the super-buoyant aquatic noodle under my foot would ricochet upward and tear off a piece of cartilage, the meniscus in my knee.

"Uh-oh," I thought, even as I reassured the therapist I was fine. My knee hadn't moved so freely since I was a girl.

Twenty-four hours later I was limping. A week later I was in my doctor's office, and the next day I was in a wheelchair looking at some gruesome X-rays with an orthopedist. The evidence was clear. A girlhood spent pounding the pavement in Keds before the high-tech shock-absorption movement hit the sneaker world had left me with half the cartilage God intended.

And, now, the meniscus—an important piece of cartilage that keeps the leg bones from scraping against each other or slipping out of place—had torn loose and was caught in the joint. Of course, the extra pounds I'd gained over the years hadn't helped—as my straight-shooting orthopedist didn't hesitate to point out. "Your knees are shot," he said succinctly as he sent me upstairs to orthopedic rehab. "You need to lose weight before you lose any more cartilage."

Sighing, I agreed. If I didn't unload the weight from my knees, my life would be a sea of pain.

The next day, I banned cheese and chips from the house and had my husband stock the frig with fish, veggies, and fruit. A low-fat oat cereal was in the cupboard.

I also went to rehab. Ann, my therapist, was an expert who had me out of the wheelchair and in a walker within an hour. She also had me doing special exercises that would strengthen my leg and help it work around the torn meniscus without damaging any more cartilage. And she encouraged me to return to my water workouts as soon as possible. They'd keep my back from getting twingy while my knee was being cranky.

By the time I headed for Kinney's drugstore to buy my own walker, Ann had given me the tools I needed to work with my injury. And the pain had given me all the motivation I needed to stick to my diet.

Neither rehab nor diet will be easy. But I come from a long line of very tough women. They made it through wars, depressions, epidemics, the death of children, and the capriciousness of men.

I can do what needs to be done.

Survival

We need to rethink priorities, simplify, and reach out a helping hand.

"I think I'm going to lose the business."

My friend looked down at her veggie wrap. She was miserable. She had worked hard for 10 years to save up and start her own business—and there'd been a lot of sacrifices along the way. But 18 months ago she'd done it. And now it was all at risk.

"We've worked so hard," she says, holding back the tears. "I'm up at 5 and in at 6 every morning. I stay every night until 7. I've thought up all kinds of promotions and community events and ways to help women in my community."

She shakes her head. "But fewer people are coming in. I'm going to have to sell my business—if I can find a buyer."

My friend—let's call her Mary—is not the only one having trouble making a buck these days. Many of us in the United States are losing jobs or seeing our hours cut—and all the while, prices on everything from food, gas, and health care are increasing by startling leaps and bounds. For Sale signs dot our neighborhoods, potholes remain unrepaired, community food shelves are empty, and we find ourselves saying "Maybe next year" to our kids about a whole host of things.

"Maybe next year we can afford a trip to Grandma's."

"Maybe next year we can see the Red Sox."

"Maybe next year we can afford those jeans."

And it's not just in the United States. Global economists have noted an economic slowdown in Germany, France, Britain, and Japan—and friends from South Africa tell me things aren't all that super there, either.

While the nasty blend of politics and greed that have caused this economic turmoil demand political solutions and a crash course in ethics, there are some things we can do to survive that, in the long run, will actually strengthen our families and our communities.

After talking with some of my friends, for example, I realize that I need to rethink my priorities.

Does my family really need two cars? Probably not. And with one car and a limited amount of time, I'll organize my travel route more efficiently. So I'll save a bazillion gallons of gas. That means I'll save serious money and reduce my country's dependence on foreign oil.

I also need to simplify. I'm mortified by how quickly cellphones, PDAs, imported balsamic vinegars, Hobo handbags, tickets to Disney World, and microwave dinners have taken over my life. How did that happen? It violates my faith. From now on, anything I buy will be frisked for both the distance it traveled to get to me and its frivolity. Is it necessary? Does it have a cheaper alternative? Did it take a barrel of foreign oil to get it to me? Does my friend Linda have one I can borrow?

I should also connect with local farmers. Aside from a zillion farmstands along the roads, there are more than 4,000 farmers' markets in urban areas of the United States alone. Buying from them not only will give me fresher foods rich in nutrients, it's likely to be cheaper as chain stores raise their prices (6 percent in one year!) in response to increased long-distance transportation costs.

I'll also help others where I can. In fact, that's something all of us need to do. We need to watch out for the old, the young, and those who can't speak for themselves. If we see someone who's hungry, we need to feed her. We can just double our homemade lasagna one night and drop it off. If we see someone who can't get up, we need to give her a helping hand. We need to take her home, find her a shelter, get her some help.

What could be more important?

The Courage to Change

Think you're too old to change? Think again.

Sitting in front of my woodstove with a book in her lap, a cup of tea in her hands, and a couple of terriers sound asleep at her feet, my 88-year-old aunt seems content to watch the season's first snowflakes drift by the window and settle on the wood stacked outside on the deck.

"Want another cookie?" I ask.

She hesitates, shakes her head no, then looks up at me with a faint twinkle in her rheumy eyes. "No—but I'll take a slice of that almond cake you made."

Smiling, I get up to slice the cake.

The trip to my cottage in the mountains of Vermont had been difficult for my aunt. And it had nothing to do with the weather or the terrain. It was because leaving her home in Pennsylvania and moving to an apartment near my cottage in Vermont had required a fiercely independent woman to lower a lifetime of barriers she had built between herself and the rest of the world. It also required that she open herself to new experiences, allow herself to be vulnerable, and, by entering into a closer relationship with me, risk confirming what she had suspected all along—that somehow she was innately unlovable.

It was a suspicion she'd harbored since childhood. She was my mother's younger sister, and to hear her tell it, she had spent her childhood completely in my mother's shadow. "It was hard coming behind her in school," my aunt once confided. "Your mother was always so quick and so bright. I was slow. The teachers…" She hesitated.

"The teachers noticed?" I asked gently.

Slowly she nodded her head. "They weren't very nice."

Nor, apparently, was her father. Decades after she'd overheard him talking to one of her teachers, she could recall his words verbatim. "He said I wasn't wanted. He said they had only wanted the one."

Her grief was palpable.

From what I can piece together, my aunt spent years trying to gain love and acceptance by molding herself into the perfect daughter (obedient, quick, intelligent), the perfect lady (demure, ankles crossed, sheets ironed), and the perfect worker (efficient, analytical, loyal).

But she was playing to the wrong crowd. Except for my mother, whose love my aunt's jealousy wouldn't allow her to accept, and except during a brief marriage that ended with the death of her husband, no one seemed to love her the way every one of us deserves.

Placing the almond cake and a napkin on the table beside her, I looked down at the frail gray head and realized that the only way she had survived was to build walls around her that no one could penetrate. She had pushed people away by criticizing or ignoring them and had brushed aside every helping hand. If no one cared about her, her rigid back seemed to say, that was OK. She didn't need them.

But then she got old, she got weak, she got forgetful, and keeping her independence depended on learning to accept help.

It was hard. At first, she'd prefer to lurch off curbs into traffic rather than take someone's arm. She'd starve rather than ask someone to pick up a nutritional supplement at the supermarket. She'd lose money rather than have someone take a look at her investments.

But slowly, as her investments shrank, her weight dropped, and her walking grew uncertain, my aunt began to realize that she had to change.

It took nine years. But gradually, day by day, she learned to lower the walls that had protected her. Not completely, mind you. But enough so that my dogs and I could jump over and surround her with love.

Today I watch as she carefully spreads the napkin on her lap and explains to the hopeful dogs at her feet that, if they're good, she just might save them a bite—and I realize that I no longer believe that people can't change. They can. No matter what their age, they can remodel themselves and start over. They can open themselves to new experiences, allow themselves to be vulnerable, and learn to take risks.

Now, sitting quietly beside my woodstove, my aunt has everything she's ever wanted in life—a warm fire, a cup of tea, a good book, sweet dogs, and a loving family that knows what she's worth.

An Iowa Perspective

A lesson from the heartland.

Pulling on an old pair of sneakers, some cutoffs, a T-shirt, and a pair of purple workout gloves, Rita Teater, a lifelong Iowa girl from down near Unionville, heads out across the lawn to the lean-to.

There she eyes Big Green, the humongous riding mower she used to cut grass until the price of gas headed for the stratosphere. Then she eyes Big Green's little brother: an old-fashioned reel mower that cost a lot less than Big Green and doesn't cost a dime to use.

Guess which one she pulls out to cut the grass?

"This is a good season in our country's history to sit back and gain a healthy perspective on things," says Rita. "The town in which I work—Centerville—is a quiet little community of about 5,500 people, and we've been hit hard by economic setbacks. Our biggest employer—it made plastic bags for Tyson foods—laid off 100 people last year and another 50 this past May. Another company, Rubbermaid, employed 500 people. They closed their doors and pulled out of town all together. Another company, a small one that made muzzle-loader rifles, sold out and moved to Georgia."

She shakes her head. "They employed 60 people."

The surrounding farms have been hit just as bad, adds Rita. With all the storms coming through during the spring planting season, it was just too wet to put in crops. Centerville didn't flood like the rest of Iowa, but it was wet. So the farmers are a month behind in the growing season—and whether or not Mother Nature will let them catch up and make any money this year is debatable.

"People are a bit tense," Rita admits.

But Rita comes from a town where people remember what it is to go through hard times. So, now, "I think back to the things my mom did as a poor farm wife to cut corners—slicing bread so thin you could read through it, and putting buttermilk in the well instead of a refrigerator."

Those lessons come in handy. And when a friend gave her a subscription to an organic magazine and she saw an ad for the reel mower, she knew what to do. "I figured I could save a lot of money," she explains. "We have half an acre to mow, and that rider mower cost me $5 every time I cut the grass.

"I did a little research and thought, This should be a piece of cake!"

"My husband," she chuckles, "told me I was on my own."

But Rita had done her homework. Now, even though she works all day at the *Curves* health club she owns in Centerville, two evenings a week she pulls on her grass-cutting clothes and workout gloves and heads out to the lean-to.

"Even though I work out, it took a little longer than I expected," she says. "Now, if I mow every 5 days, I can mow the whole thing in about 2 ½ hours. The reel mower gives a better cut than Big Green, and the whole place smells like fresh-cut grass. Not only do I save $5 a week in gas, but pushing that mower for a few hours burns off at *least* 500 calories.

"Big Green is terminal," she adds. "Its battery is dead."

Faith @ Home

Faith is alive and well all across America.
But it's no longer limited to a building topped by a steeple.

Moving to the edge of her farmhouse's porch in upstate New York, Spee Braun can look out over a countryside tangled with wildflowers and literally see her faith taking shape.

A fifth-generation Christian Quaker who has worked for Save the Children since graduate school—serving most recently as a trouble-shooter in Iraq—Spee and her husband, Jens, a former consultant on international development, are building an "intentional" village—a tiny community for themselves and several other families who want to integrate faith more deeply into their home life. Two houses, both of which structurally incorporate Quaker values of simplicity and respect for nature, have already been built; a third is under way.

"Our purpose is to grow closer to God," says Spee comfortably. "Once the houses are complete and the other families have moved onto the land, we'll probably meet for silent worship every day and rotate worship from one house to another."

As Spee and Jens's plans suggest, religious faith is taking on a new shape in the United States. Studies show that somewhere around 177 million Americans claim a religious affiliation—and some 20 percent of us actually hit the pews, benches, and prayer rugs on a regular basis.

That percentage isn't much different from when this country was founded, says Brent Bill, executive vice president of Indianapolis's

Center for Congregations. What *is* different, however, is that while today's faithful may still worship the same God as their parents, grand-parents, and great-grandparents, many may be as likely to do it at home as in a neighborhood church, synagogue, or mosque.

"Practicing faith at home is hot," says religion researcher Cynthia Woolever, Ph.D., a professor of sociology and religious organization at Hartford Seminary in Connecticut, who has surveyed hundreds of thousands of the faithful across the country. The trend is fueled in part by a growing sense of wanting a deeper, more authentic faith that will bring people closer to God.

That speaks to the Brauns in a big way—and they've put their own creative twist on it by actually incorporating their religious principles of simplicity and respect for the earth into the very walls of their house.

Rather than build something entirely new with fiberglass roof tiles from China and nails from southeast Asia, they restored what they could of an old structure, then used "green" local materials to create a house that they could build and fix themselves. Instead of fiberglass insula-tion in the walls, for example, Jens poured wood chips into a foot-thick frame and plastered it with clay on the outside.

It was a hot, sweaty, dirty, backbreaking job, but by the time he was done, the chip-and-plaster walls had the equivalent of R-30 insulation.

Now, when Spee, Jens, or one of their kids sits on the porch to sip a cool glass of water from their own well, the sturdy warmth of their home, the purity of the water, and the sun shining through a landscape that supports deer, bear, birds, and an abundance of wildlife reminds them of God's grace upon the earth.

"Our thinking is that there is that of God within every one of us, and in everything around us," says Jens as he looks out over the landscape.

"Here, our intention is to live that truth every day."

Are You Living the Life You Were Meant to Live?

Sometimes it seems as if the dirty laundry and unpaid bills of life are conspiring to keep us from a life of meaning and purpose.

Swinging her boat across the sunny wind-whipped waves crashing into a bay on Vermont's Lake Champlain, 40-year-old Holly Poulin tugs the "Driftwood Tours" baseball cap down snugly over her sun-streaked hair and, with a twist of her wrist, sends the 21-foot craft into the calmer waters off Hibbard's Point.

"There," she says calmly. "That's better."

She smiles as I let out the deep breath I've been holding since we left the dock. Cautiously, I look at the turbulent green water around me, then at the amused boat captain beside me. While I'm barely one leap from the cache of lifejackets in the bow, Holly is in her element. Head up, one hand draped over the wheel, eyes constantly reading the waves ahead, body rhythmically riding the swells, she casually angles the boat through each wave so that we move steadily toward the Point.

"You love it out here, don't you?" I ask.

Holly looks at me, her tanned face relaxed, her gray-green eyes reflecting the water. "I was meant to be here," she says simply.

As Holly gently eases her boat up to the dock, I suddenly wonder just how many of us could actually stand up and claim that we're where we were meant to be, doing what we were meant to do.

Once most of my friends hit the ground running in our twenties, we all thought we were heading straight toward our destiny. We worked 437 hours a week, networked ourselves comatose on weekends, found someone to love, gave birth, moved into less housing than we needed at prices more expensive than we could afford, then started running faster than ever.

And that worked for a while. But then somewhere in our 30s or 40s, some of us looked around and realized that we had been running down the wrong path.

Unfortunately, by the time most of us have figured out who we are, where we're supposed to be, and what we're supposed to be doing, it seems as if the dirty laundry and unpaid bills of life are conspiring to keep us from a life of meaning and purpose—and the sheer *weight* of the lives we've built seems to hold us in place.

Fortunately, that doesn't mean we have to stay there.

My friend Holly is a perfect example. Holly grew up on Lake Champlain and assumed that she'd spend the rest of her life fishing, boating, swimming, and exploring its 587 miles of shoreline.

But somewhere along the line, she met a guy and set up house-keeping far from the sound of waves. When, about 15 years ago, she recognized that she was in the wrong place, with the wrong man, on the wrong path, she packed up her then-three-year-old son, Ben, and left.

She had no skills, no money, and she needed flexible hours to be available to Ben. So she started cleaning houses and offices.

Within 10 years, she had several dozen clients and two employees. But a cleaning business had never been what Holly wanted for herself. "Being on the lake was my dream," she says wistfully. "When I rented a place on the lake, I'd wake up in the morning and just stare at the lake and think, I know I can do something on that lake to make money. I just *know* it!"

When Ben was 13 and spending more time with his dad, Holly evaluated several possibilities and decided to start building a summer charter-boat business.

The first step was to go back to school and get her captain's license; the second was to buy a boat suitable for charters. She spent months studying tides, currents, knots, winds, and seas; passed the eight-hour exam in Boston with flying colors; then began to research boats, weighing one boat's hull against another boat's speed and stability. Finally she settled on a pontoon boat, a stable craft that rides lightly on the waves. She christened the boat *Sacajawea*.

Deciding to focus her charter business in and around a group of islands in the northern part of the lake, Holly contacted innkeepers throughout the area and offered to pick up passengers at their docks from Memorial Day through Vermont's autumn foliage season in October. The innkeepers gave her dock space—and Holly was in business.

Now, after five years or so of cruising the islands, Holly plans to ditch her cleaning business altogether, work on the lake full-time all summer, then head for Key West and start up a charter business down there.

"Timing is everything," says Holly as she ties us up at the Hibbard's Point dock. "Ben's grown. The truck's paid off. The boat's paid off. I have a mortgage on my farmhouse, but that's it. And that gives me the freedom to go down to the Keys and take a chance."

She shoves her hands in her pockets, toes a sneaker into the slated dock, looks up at the mountains surrounding the lake, then back at me.

"It's a little scary," she adds. "But it feels good." She grins. "It's what I was meant to do."

The Farm Market

The women selling flowers, hummus, and tomatoes have figured out how to be who they are.

Sitting under the huge old trees shading the village green, my friend Mattie and I watched as neighbors slowly wandered in and out of the late afternoon sun from one gaily colored tent to another—picking up a basket of jewel-red berries here, a colander of fresh-picked greens there, and stopping off under the Weed Farm's tent for a taste of "Scarborough Fair," their incredible hummus made with—what else?—parsley, sage, rosemary, and thyme.

"I'm a musician as well as a farmer," laughs Weed Farm's Sue Borg, when I ask her how she came up with the name. "What else would I name it?"

It was the Wednesday afternoon farmers' market in Bristol, Vermont, and local farmers had trucked in fresh vegetables, flowers, herbs, just-canned jars of dilly beans, farm-fresh jams, baskets of green beans, and an amazing assortment of fresh-baked cookies, pies, and breads.

The late afternoon sun slipped through overhead branches to highlight a couple of toddlers happily splashing in a small stone fountain, and two or three musicians lightly slapped their West African drums in a soft rhythmic backdrop that almost lulled us to sleep.

Women stopped by the table where Mattie and I were sitting, to ask questions about their gardens. As Master Gardeners—Mattie's actually certified by the University of Vermont, while I'm just a baby gardener-in-training—we're here to help folks deal with peonies that don't bloom, roses with blistered leaves, root-nibbling voles, tomato-loving fungi, and invasive plants brought from Europe a century ago that are now threatening to take over Vermont.

Mostly Mattie helps and I listen. Mattie is so knowledgeable, so smart, and so passionate about plants that every home gardener who approaches our table rapidly moves from confusion and befuddlement to enlightenment, clarity, and inner peace.

When you know what's got you by the carrots, says the practical Mattie, it's usually easy enough to fix.

The interaction between Mattie and our neighbors is remarkable to watch. And even more remarkable when you realize that this tiny, unassuming, carrot-topped bundle of passionate energy is actually a computational physicist—a physicist who solved complex mathematical equations for an astrophysics group at the Lawrence Berkeley National Laboratory, a government-sponsored think tank at the University of California.

"Being a woman in physics is a lonely place to be," she says in her quick, little-girl voice. "All the other women at the lab either died or quit."

After showing the guys what a woman could do, Mattie opted for quitting. It was clearly the better alternative. But no sooner was she settled in another job than she literally got hit by a truck.

"Airborne Express," she says ruefully. "It took a year to recover."

She went home to her parents in Iowa. And aside from healing—and fighting a nasty legal battle related to the accident—she taught herself computer programming languages, played around with creating websites, and did a lot of thinking.

Finally, she decided that being in control of where she lived, how she worked, and with whom she worked was what was most important.

"I decided that I wanted my own house and my own business," Mattie says.

She moved to Vermont and got both. But, courtesy of an early client of her new website development business, she also had an epiphany. "I thought he'd hired me for my skills," says Mattie. "He later told me he'd hired me because of my sense of humor! That was amazing.

"What it boiled down to," she adds, "is that I was hired for who I was, not what I could do." For someone who'd believed firmly that what she was worth was dictated by what she could do for an organization, the realization was stunning. It liberated her to explore just who she was and follow her passions in other areas—including gardening. Now, at age 47, she's thinking about going back to school for a degree in horticulture. "I'm really into compost," says Mattie irrepressibly. "I'll make ten times less money, but I'm old enough now to say that I don't much care. I'll sell my big-ass old house and buy something that costs one-tenth as much, then putter out in the garden."

Listening to Mattie's story and looking around at the women selling flowers, vegetables, and other farm products at the market, I realize that Mattie is not the only woman who has moved from one career to another as she's evolved.

Sue Borg, she of the incredible hummus, was a music teacher in the city of Burlington for years. Now she grows fresh herbs, sells her amazing hummus, and directs chorus groups in the community.

Eugenie Doyle, who owns the Last Resort farm in Monkton, is a farmer six months of the year and a novelist who writes books for teens the other six months.

And Marijke Niles, a former KLM flight attendant, went back to school, headed a dance company, directed a theater company, headed the University of Notre Dame's development program for a Shakespeare initiative—then moved to Vermont and planted a wildflower farm high in the Green Mountains that gave life to her passion for flowers. "Marijke's Perennials" are now a byword among local gardeners.

The list goes on. But if this simple farm market is any guide, few women are locked into one role, or one stage, or even one life. Instead, we allow ourselves to evolve. To be molded by life. To investigate the new. To develop passions. To hear new callings.

We are so blessed.

The New Frugality

The amazing way we're reinventing ourselves—
and really learning how to live.

Watching my friend Ann in the toy store trying to figure out if she can afford a big-lettered Rummikub game as a Father's Day gift for her dad is painful.

The elderly man is having trouble making out regular-sized letters during the Sunday night game in his senior community, and Ann knows the larger-lettered game would make a difference. But, like many of us these days, she's broke. She's been laid off, her industry is crumbling, and local businesses aren't hiring.

Her husband, Drew, has been laid off, too, and in the small town in which they live, chances are good that he won't find another job. "Even McDonald's doesn't need help," he chuckles ruefully.

The couple is grateful that Drew's unemployment compensation covers their food. His old employer has hired him back one day a week, which covers their monthly propane bill. And Ann, who has some serious health issues, got a part-time gig that covers her health insurance, phone bill, electric bill, gas for the car, credit card debt, medical copays, and medication.

But Drew has had to cancel his health insurance, and there's no money for the mortgage—$898 every month plus $350 for property taxes. In fact, the only thing that keeps Ann and Drew from sliding down the rabbit hole is the $18,000 Drew had managed to save toward their retirement, a keen sense of what's important in life—and the inventive way both Ann and Drew are using this unexpected downtime.

Studies show that American workers work harder than any other people on the planet. And Ann and Drew are no exception. Both have worked since they got out of school nearly 40 years ago. Yes, there were a few breaks to have a child or move from one job to another. But for the most part, they kept their noses to the proverbial grindstone and worked their butts off to pay off their college loans, afford a house, have a baby, and then send their kid to college.

But now, even though they're still actively looking for work, for the first time in their lives, they've got some downtime.

"At first, it was disorienting," says Ann. "I'd wake up in the morning, make some coffee, check job listings on the Internet, make some calls, then just kind of putter around. After I'd cleaned up the kitchen, there was really nothing to do."

Drew was in the same position. But for years he'd been working on environmental issues in their community as a volunteer. He'd had an idea that could really make a difference in cleaning up their state's air, but he'd never really had the time to build an organization that could put it into effect. Now he did. So every day after he'd checked the online want ads, he spent hours at the computer and on the phone—pulling together research and people into an organization that will have a significant impact on our health.

Ann, after several months spent networking, revising her résumé, and driving Drew crazy, eventually got busy, too. "I come from a long line of coupon clippers," Ann admits, "and I was determined to figure out something that would save me dollars as well as cents."

Pretty soon she began swapping things with friends and neighbors— garden compost in exchange for use of a pickup, fruit pies in exchange for blackberry root cuttings, homemade applesauce in exchange for some old canning jars. So far her biggest score has been to swap an ergonomic office chair she wasn't using for free income-tax preparation from a local CPA—a savings of $350.

"The one thing I couldn't get a handle on was our grocery bill," says Ann. "But when fresh string beans hit $3 a pound at my supermarket, I knew it was time to grow my own."

Ann had been planting gardens for years, but she never really knew what she was doing. She'd get lucky with beans but lose all her tomatoes. Or helplessly watch the lettuce get eaten by bugs. So this time, as a Christmas present, Drew reached into his retirement savings and paid for a Master Gardener course at their local state university.

It wasn't cheap. But three months later, with lectures from plant and soil scientists under her belt and a network of other Master Gardeners to call upon for advice, Ann put in a huge garden that, once its vegetables are properly canned or frozen, will feed her family for the whole winter, God and nematodes willing.

What's more, she's turned her new skills to helping others. Several days a week she shows up at a local nursing home to work with elderly, wheelchair-bound gardeners—mostly women. With a hand here and a gentle touch there, the gardeners sow seeds, transplant seedlings, weed, mulch, water, swap remedies for tomato blight or vole attacks, and pick flowers for their rooms.

"I never dreamed helping an older gardener touch the soil or hold a sweet pea against her cheek could be so moving," says Ann.

"Who would've thought not having enough money to eat could bring such a blessing?"

Women Who Ride the Dragon

A community demonstrates its fierce support
of women with breast cancer.

Tall, blond, and tanned by a summer on the open water, 55-year-old Linda Dwyer stood at the community boat launch on Vermont's Lake Champlain, a two-way radio in one hand, a cell in the other.

Huge thunderstorm clouds dropped dangerously toward the water, almost obscuring the Adirondack peaks lining the western side of the lake. Torrents of rain drenched both shores, from the Canadian border south to the waterfront where Linda monitored volunteer dockworkers preparing 40-foot-long dragon boats—long, narrow canoe-style boats with elaborately carved dragon heads and tails—to race.

In precisely timed waves, whole boatloads of firefighters, breast cancer survivors, radiologists, bankers, electricians, ER workers, teachers, hairdressers, lawyers, nurses, and construction workers donned life vests, grabbed their paddles, and clattered down the dock to their boats. Boats were steadied, lines cast off, and every seven minutes a dragon boat with a steersman, 20-person crew of laughing but competitive paddlers, and a drummer to keep them in sync left the dock and headed out into the lake's choppy water for the starting line.

"Aren't they incredible?" asked Linda as she paused beside me.

The oversized baseball cap that shielded her face from the rain couldn't hide the sheer joy that glowed from every cell in her body as

2,000 paddlers—13 teams of breast cancer survivors from all over the United States and Canada, plus 81 teams of community supporters—passed by us to compete for medals and raise money for two organizations: Vermont's Breast Cancer Patient Emergency Services Fund, and Dragonheart Vermont, the breast cancer survivor paddling organization that Linda and her husband, local basketball coach John Dwyer, had put together over the past four years. Dragonheart was also the organizer of today's Dragon Boat Festival on Lake Champlain.

By the end of the day, $160,000 had been raised, an entire community had demonstrated its fierce support of women with breast cancer, and those who had fought and survived the disease had celebrated their strength, their spirit, their connection—and the fact that they were clearly more than ready to kick butt in the upcoming international races on their schedule.

"Incredible" just isn't the word.

Not long ago, exercise for breast cancer survivors was an anathema. Women who had had breast cancer were often told after surgery that they shouldn't participate in sports, shouldn't exercise, shouldn't carry more than 15 pounds, shouldn't lift their arms, shouldn't even sling a handbag over their shoulder. The fear was that repetitive upper body exercise would trigger lymphedema, a painful continuing condition in which lymph fluid collects in the arm and chest wall as a result of damage during surgery or radiation.

Today that's changed. A Canadian doctor at the University of British Columbia who specializes in sports medicine, Don McKenzie, challenged the conventional wisdom in 1996 and launched the first breast cancer survivor dragon boat team. Now a huge multi-center study from researchers at Yale School of Medicine reveals that women with breast cancer who engage in two to three hours of brisk exercise each week reduced their risk of death by a whopping *45 percent.*

The study's findings make sense to 77-year-old Shirley Lane, a breast cancer survivor who paddles on the Dragonheart team and works out at the local South Burlington *Curves* fitness center.

Sitting in the tent of Dragon Boat Festival sponsor Ben & Jerry's after the morning's races, Shirley, a Eucharistic minister for her church, reminds me that the women who paddle dragon boats have gotten more than a better chance at their four score and ten—they've also taken a poke at that ever-present fear of recurrence that haunts every survivor.

"It's been 28 years since I was diagnosed with breast cancer," Shirley says, "and the fear of recurrence is still in the back of my mind. But when I get through paddling, the adrenaline is pouring out of me and I'm like, *'Bring it on!' I can do anything!"*

Dragonheart founder Linda Dwyer chuckles when she hears Shirley's words. "It's exhilarating to be out there," she admits, nodding toward the water. "It's especially meaningful for a breast cancer survivor to hop in that boat and sit next to other breast cancer survivors. There's an immediate connection. You feel each other's heart pounding. You feel each woman's power as the boat moves forward. You feel the boat take off.

"Cancer is an isolating disease," she adds. *"This* is pure joy."

Sitting in one of the team tents while team members attend the festival's awards ceremony, I'm thinking about Linda's words as retired Christmas tree farmer Mary Ann Castimore stops by.

"Every one of us knows someone who's no longer in the boat with us," says Mary Ann, a breast cancer survivor whose cancer metastasized 13 years ago. "And everyone knows that one of us might not be here next year. That said, just look at this group of women." She gestures to a dragon boat team laughing, talking, and waving to friends as they head toward their team tent.

I look.

And I remember what breast cancer survivor Pam Blum told me just hours ago: "Most of us thought our lives were over when we got diagnosed.

"The message here is that life has just begun."

How Much Is Enough?

It's a pivotal question. Asking it gave one Maryland
music teacher her dream.

Twirling across the richly polished floor of her log home, my friend
Mary quietly gives commands to the massive golden Labrador retriever
who is twirling across the room with her.

The two are breathtakingly beautiful. The morning sun shines
through a picture window framing the distant Adirondack Mountains,
lightly slides over Mary's sun-streaked hair, and is irretrievably caught in
the dog's silky golden coat as they move.

The retriever's head is always 2 inches from Ann's thigh no matter in
which direction she pivots or how fast she moves. Suddenly she stops
near the fireplace, commands "Front!," and Murphy, the beautiful two-
year-old with whom she's been working, instantly moves in front of her
and sits.

The bond between the two is unmistakable. After praising his efforts,
Mary looks up at me and laughs. "I think he's earned a treat, don't you?"

She heads for the treat jar with Murphy barely a heartbeat behind,
then settles down with me to a plate of blueberry scones and a cup of tea
at the old dining-room table she loves. A wall clock chimes as Murphy
ducks under the table and sprawls on a small rug, his big beautiful head
resting on my feet.

"Oh, that's good," Mary sighs after her first bite.

At 55, Mary has learned to appreciate the simple things in life. A light scone, spinach fresh from her garden, a challenging hike, a beautiful dog.

She gets up every morning around 5:00 A.M., tucks the covers around her husband, Ben, checks to see if any deer are wandering around outside her home in the Vermont mountains, and bustles about until it is time to meet her friend Nancy at the beginning of the Jerusalem Trail down the road.

The trail cuts straight up the mountain on which the women live, and there's nothing the two enjoy more than hiking the trail straight up to an old logging road, then following it along the mountain until it descends toward a track that leads back to the road on which they live. The women chatter happily as Murphy and Nancy's dog, Zeke—also a golden retriever—splash across nearby brooks and race through the trees as they follow the rich scents of grouse, deer, bear, and moose.

Once Mary and Murphy are back home, life is filled with digging in the garden, working on sewing projects, hours of violin practice, duets with her friend Molly, testing out recipes from America's Test Kitchen, and performing in a regional orchestra.

Mary tickles Murphy's belly under the table with her toes and smiles. It's a life that she's worked hard to get.

For 17 years, she worked as an instrumental music teacher in the often troubled schools of a Maryland suburb. When she started, she was assigned to five schools and was expected to run back and forth among them.

The stress was toxic. One week "I had a concert Monday afternoon and Monday evening in one school, a concert Wednesday afternoon and Wednesday evening in another," says Mary. "Running back and forth between the two schools, I fell asleep in a Wendy's parking lot. And the next day I came down with hives." She finished out the week with a final exam for a master's degree course on Thursday and two more student concerts on Friday.

She still can't believe she did it. But, eventually, Mary got her master's degree and grew the music programs in her schools. That earned her more students but in fewer schools—and gave her the "extra" time she needed to serve as president of the Maryland Orchestra Association.

But, unfortunately, between her job and Ben's, the two were working 12 hours a day. And Ben traveled.

"We'd see each other on Saturday mornings." Mary chuckles. "We had this dream of one day building a log home complete with gourmet kitchen. So we'd wake up on Saturday morning, have coffee and breakfast in bed, and watch these log home shows on TV."

The two of them were making good money, but their work schedules were forcing them into leading separate lives. What both eventually realized was that they wanted simpler lives—and they wanted their lives to be together. So the two sat down and asked themselves, *"How much is enough?"*

It took a lot of thought. But, gradually, the couple began to separate needs from wants, necessities from luxuries, the important from the unimportant. "You can always work more and earn more," Mary reasoned, "but you have to decide if it's worth the price."

It wasn't long before the two of them had a plan in place. They would live modestly, save their pennies, invest them wisely, and Ben would retire at 55. Mary, who was two years younger, would retire at 53. The two would buy land somewhere in New England, where Mary had grown up, and they would build their log home. Then Ben would retire, play golf, and cook stuffed mushrooms for their friends. Mary would spend time playing the violin, gardening, and working with him in the kitchen.

A couple of times their plan got sideswiped. Ben, who was a government worker, had his retirement canceled because of 9/11 and had to work a few years longer than planned. And last year Mary was diagnosed with breast cancer. Between radiation and a botched hysterectomy, she spent a lot of time focusing on putting one foot in front of the other and fighting the overwhelming fatigue that comes with cancer.

But that's all behind them now. Today Ben is tooling his tractor through his mountain meadow and Mary is hiking the 272-mile Long Trail that stretches across the spine of the Green Mountains from Massachusetts to Canada. She's put the cancer behind her, the fatigue is beginning to recede, and the delightful personality that her friends treasure is once again skipping around the entire neighborhood.

Today, says Mary, with a glance at the heap of golden fur under the table, "I'm trying to learn from my dog. He walks. He sleeps. He eats. He's happy."

She looks up, and her laughter flows through the room. "I am *so* richly blessed!"

A Celebration of Friends & Family

Blessed are they who have the gift of making friends,
for it is one of God's best gifts. It involves many things,
but above all, the power of getting out of one's self and
appreciating whatever is noble and loving in another.

—Thomas Hughes, 19th-century social reformer

A Garden for My Mother

*Gently touching the pages of my mother's old gardening book
and lightly tracing her penciled notes with a finger,
the grief I felt at her absence was palpable.*

Pirouetting across the barren, scarred ground in front of my cottage high in the mountains of Vermont, my friend Sylvia was clearly delighted with the challenge I'd handed her.

Last winter, 93-mile-an-hour winds had ripped a whole stand of tall pine trees out of the ground. The rich forest floor had disappeared in the storm's turbulent aftermath, and only the packed clay subsoil, marked by the treads of a log truck, tractor, and an excavator, remained.

Sylvia, a garden designer at the local nursery, was thrilled.

"We can put a pagoda dogwood over there," she beamed, pointing her sketchbook toward an area that had, until last December, contained 15 pine trees and the rich, nurturing soil of a pine forest.

"We can put a birch clump over there." She pointed with her pen. "And a holly over there." The sketchbook gestured in the opposite direction.

"And can we move the Japanese lantern?"

Quirking a questioning eyebrow at me, she paused a moment as I sat on the cottage's front steps and considered. "We can put it here in front of that remaining hemlock, with a weeping pea tree," she clarified. "With a tall sheaf of Japanese silvergrass and a 6-inch-high waterfall of white pine that wanders through the arrangement." Her hands sketched the plants and their placement as she talked.

"What do you think?"

Sylvia's plan was perfect. At my sudden smile and nod of agreement, the designer whirled toward the hemlock, her bright red coat flaring out in the spring sunshine. The visions inside her head tumbled onto her sketchpad at a rapid rate—and I knew it wouldn't be long before those visions would reclaim the storm-roughened ground in front of us.

Leaving Sylvia to finish plotting out square feet and plant sizes, I went inside the cottage to look through my gardening books and check out the plants she'd suggested.

What on earth was a weeping pea tree, anyway? Running my fingers along a bookshelf of colorful book covers bursting with exotic flowers and shaggy barks, I stopped at one old book, its plain green cover darkened by age. Pages torn from a desk calendar that my mother used back in 1972—with notes in her perfect British schoolgirl penmanship about specific plants—were inserted among the pages.

The book had been hers. Every spring she'd pull it out, sit down at the kitchen table to study it, and mark the plants she wanted on pages from the calendar:

April 20th: "*Hypericum 'Hidcote'. 5 feet. Elegant.*"

April 21st: "*Magnolia. Large saucer-shaped flowers.*"

April 25th: "*Ilex opaca, an American holly.*"

April 26th: "*Forsythia 'Lynwood Gold',*
large flowers with broad petals."

May 25th: "*Weigela. Spring-flowering shrubs, which bear*
trumpet-shaped flowers in great abundance..."

May 28th: "*Syringa lilacs. 8 to 12 feet. Flower in the spring...*"

The book would sit on the table for weeks until, recognizing she couldn't afford everything she wanted, she'd put it back on the bookshelf. "Next year," she'd say. "Next year we'll plant the magnolia"—or the lilac or the forsythia or whatever else had caught her fancy.

But looking over the list of plants from her 1972 notes, I realized that she'd never planted any of them. It was the year my father had retired from the navy, and money was scarce. By the following spring she had had a heart attack and—those being the days when cardiac rehab was pretty much rest, blood thinners, and lectures on smoking cigarettes—she gave up her cigarettes, gave up her garden, and moved with my father to Florida for a less-expensive, less-active life.

She died there six years later.

Gently touching the pages of her old gardening book and lightly tracing her penciled notes with a finger, the grief I felt at her absence was palpable. She'd never seen her grandson grow into a strong, caring man. Never seen her daughter become a loving, nurturing woman. Never planted her magnolia. Never closed her eyes in bliss as a light spring breeze brought the scent of lilacs into the house.

Thoughtfully, I looked out the window at Sylvia making her sketches, then looked down at my mother's notes.

Adding a magnolia, some lilacs, a graceful fountain of forsythia, and a patch of cheerful yellow hypericum to Sylvia's design might not be a bad idea. It would create a small cottage garden that would fill the space in front of my home and—perhaps—fill that small space in my heart that holds the woman who made me do the dishes, taught me how to make mud pies, and loved me fiercely.

Closing my mother's book, I got up to go talk with Sylvia.

It was past time for Mama to have her garden.

Love in a Pyrex Bowl

When a neighbor dies, an entire community gathers to hold
those left behind in its love.

Putting the fresh green romaine leaves on my kitchen cutting board, I
reach for the huge chef's knife and begin to chop. Two minutes later the
crisp leaves join a huge pile of chopped carrots, broccoli, cauliflower,
and green beans, and I reach for the cherry tomatoes.

I was making a salad for my neighbors. One of them down the road,
a 62-year-old guy with a great sense of humor, had developed pancreatic
cancer. After a long, heartbreaking struggle, he had succumbed to the
disease. His family—a wife, mother, brother, sister, children, in-laws,
and cousins—were bereft.

Thinking about them, I sighed. His brother Greg was a friend of
ours who lived a couple of curves away—a warm, caring neighbor who
was on your doorstep when anyone needed help. Car stuck in a rut? He
got out his chains. Road washed out by a storm? He was in a front-end
loader moving dirt around before you knew you were stranded. Wor-
ried about town maintenance? He could tell you how to show respect
for the old Vermonters, navigate town politics, and get things done. But
how could anyone help him? Or any of his family? How could any of us
soothe away the pain of watching a beloved brother, father, cousin, and
friend die? How could anyone comfort his amazing wife?

I reached for the red cabbage, sliced it in half, then began to chop again. When my father had died some years before, every one of my beloved stepmother's friends had baked a cake or bought a pie and brought it over. We were awash in lemon chiffon, angel food, gooey cherries, and chocolate cream from the Piggly Wiggly. There was nary a casserole or pan of lasagna to give us strength, no plate of fresh fruit to refresh our souls, no veggies to keep our bodies nourished and our immune systems functioning. Instead, we had mountains of sugar to speed us up, shake us around, and drop us in a heap.

I pulled a chunk of Parmesan out of the refrigerator, slipped off the wrapper, and began to grate it over the bowl. I understood the sugar. To my stepmother's friends, every cake, every pie, every calorie-laden bite was a message of love, a hand to hold, a great big hug. My salad worked the same way.

Reaching for the balsamic and a bottle of light olive oil, I sprinkled both over the salad, tossed it lightly until it glistened, and covered the huge glass salad bowl with a sheet of clear plastic. My husband stood by, ready to carry it to our neighbor's. Eventually, it would arrive at the local Baptist church, where the funeral was to be held. There, in a tiny church nestled in a small country village of maybe three dozen houses, a school, a store, a library, and surrounding farms, my salad would sit on tables loaded with literally hundreds of other dishes as an entire community—more than 300 strong—gathered to hold those left behind in its love.

The bringing of food to a funeral is, author Michael Lee West points out, "…concern and sympathy in a Pyrex bowl. It is humanity at its finest."

I am so blessed to live here.

The Lady

There is only one incredible woman who deserves the title—
the incredible Alyce.

"Old age *sucks!*" says my mother-in-law as she crouches over the Scrabble board, stabs a finger at the nosepiece of her red plastic glasses, and shoves them back into place. *"But…!"* she says emphatically as, one letter at a time, she decisively snaps down a seven-letter word: H-E-A-V-E-N-S.

Her son, my beloved husband, just groans.

"I win!" she cackles, throwing up her arms in the age-old symbol of victory.

My husband hangs his head in mock defeat.

Approaching her 100th birthday, Alyce Emuryan Michaud—"The Lady," as we call her—is something of a wonder. Her smooth skin is virtually unlined. There are few age spots. Her lipstick is bright red, her eyelids smudged with shadow, and her carefully colored black hair is drawn back in the same elegant coiffure she's worn for 50 years.

The exterior is as beautiful as it has always been. But, as all of her kids sense, the inside is crumbling. The great heart that has powered the diminutive woman from an Armenian village on Asia Minor to a court-yarded condo in one of Philadelphia's most affluent suburbs is failing.

The strong oxlike bones that have kept her back straight, her head upright, and her chin tilted at a proud, arrogant angle for nearly 100 years are thinning.

The fine, nuanced mind—stimulated by well-educated parents, challenged by equally bright brothers, honed at the University of Pennsylvania in her teens—now has difficulty finding words, forming sentences, and accepting any opinion other than her own.

Her indomitable spirit—forged in the early years of the 20th century as she grew up Christian and Armenian in a nation that is both Muslim and Turk—can now only carry her through turmoil in short bursts.

And her voice—once a thing of great beauty as she sang achingly lovely songs of love and despair for audiences in Philadelphia and New York—is a joyous but unreliable instrument as it deconstructs a Scrabble word, holds forth on politics, or describes a soap-opera villain with equal relish.

Watching her from across the table as she and my husband argue about whether or not "cutesy" is a word, I can already sense her leaving. Slowly, inexorably, day by day, hour by hour, minute by minute, she is withdrawing. She sleeps a little more, rises a little later, gets tired a little more quickly.

One day, in the not-too-distant future, she'll be gone. That tiny body, which I tucked under my arm on my wedding day, will no longer be energized by the indomitable spirit that has compelled her to remain independent for so long. It will no longer offer the great love she has shown her family as they argued and split and healed and re-formed. It will no longer provide the solid anchor that has kept us all firmly grounded.

But looking at the sparkle in her eyes as she trounces my husband yet again at Scrabble—and listening to her raucous laughter as she enjoys it so thoroughly—I sense that she will stay long enough to give us the opportunity to give back a little of what she has given us. To paint her toenails scarlet, cook her linguine and clams, and mulch her roses against the coming winter. To hold her in our arms as she has held each of us.

And that is a blessing.

Traveling with Pots

Staying connected with friends and family scattered
around the globe is tough.

Swinging the zippered boat bag up onto the airport security counter, I cautiously eyed the TSA agent behind it.

I was flying out to visit my son, Matthew, in Los Angeles. He was working 24/7 to develop a film, had split with a longtime girlfriend, and had just moved to an apartment on Venice Beach. He sounded fine, but there was a lot on his plate, and my maternal instincts were on high alert.

I wasn't going to interfere. Or advise. Or empathize. Or ask a single question. My son was a highly intelligent 26-year-old who made good decisions. I was simply going for one of my periodic visits. With my pots.

The TSA agent picked up the boat bag and, surprised at its weight, gave me a sharp look.

I smiled back innocently. I'm a mother. I don't do crime, at least not unless someone threatens my child.

Keeping his eyes on mine, the agent plunked the bag down on a steel examining table.

If you knew what was in the bag, the metallic thud came as no surprise. If you didn't...well, you didn't like it. The agent's eyes narrowed and he stepped back a pace. "Don't move," he warned as he signaled a colleague forward, pointed at me, and reached for his two-way radio.

Oh, God. This was going to get embarrassing.

"It's a soup pot!" I blurted nervously.

As the two agents stood ready to make sure I didn't produce any other deadly weapons, another TSA agent scanned the bag, chuckled, then passed it to a fourth, who opened it up. After a thorough examination and a few mortifying taps that made the pot ring like a dinner bell throughout the airport screening area, the agent zipped the bag shut, tossed it on the baggage conveyer belt, and nodded his OK to the agents standing beside me.

"She's clear. It *is* a pot. A big one."

The agents beside me were apologetic. "Sorry, ma'am. Just trying to be careful," said one.

"I know. And I appreciate that," I reassured him. "Would you like one of my brownies? They're in the other bag."

Traveling with pots may seem a bit eccentric if you're not Paula Deen or Rachael Ray, but it's something that I do fairly often. There's just something in me that loves to feed family, friends, neighbors—anyone, I guess, who doesn't move away fast enough.

My aunt Ellen regularly fed the entire University of South Carolina football squad when her grandsons were on the team. So maybe it's genetic. Or maybe it's a leftover response from all those church potlucks and casseroles I grew up on. If someone had a baby, you brought a week's supply of frozen casseroles for their family. If someone moved into a new house, you left a cookie jar stuffed with blondies on their front porch. If someone was sick, you hauled over a big pot of soup, stuck it on the stove, and called their kids for dinner.

You tried to help out, reach out, and comfort where you could. When the daughter of my son's kindergarten teacher unexpectedly died, all 18 of us class moms got together and brought dinner to that woman and her husband every night until the funeral, then weekly thereafter for a year.

In some instinctual, prehistoric, totally primitive way, food connects us to one another. Cell phones and webcams are all well and good, and instant messaging is a blessing. But all those marvelous technologies lack warmth and texture. My soups—especially the rich broth made from simmering a fresh free-range chicken with a handful of sea salt and 10 cloves of fresh garlic for 7 hours—have it in abundance.

The Ladies of North Coventry

Sometimes all you need is a little help from your friends.

Sitting surrounded by a half-dozen friends on deck 10 of the cruise ship *Empress of the Seas,* Ginger Miller was talking about the months since her husband had died.

"He was sick for so long," she says regretfully. "Thirteen years." She looks out over the sunny ocean and sighs. "The last five years were hard."

Ginger doesn't elaborate, but anyone who has been forced to watch as a beloved friend or relative struggled with terminal cancer knows something about what she experienced. Cancer can be a heartbreaking disease, and for those who care for the people in its last stages, the work is backbreaking. The nights are long, the days longer, treatments fail, prayers go seemingly unanswered, and, in the end, there doesn't seem to be a thing you can do to make anything better—for you or the person you love.

Fortunately, Ginger had friends—a whole pack of them in an exercise group at the local North Coventry *Curves* fitness club in Pennsylvania. And today that's just who's jamming the tables around us on the ship's luxurious top-deck restaurant. Talking constantly, waving their hands expressively, tablehopping, and laughing, the women looked and sounded more like a group of high-energy junior high girls at lunchtime in a school cafeteria than mature women on a cruise to Bermuda.

"It's a great group," says Ginger as she looks at the women around us with a slow smile. "After my husband died, I'd get up in the morning and be all alone. So I started going to *Curves* at 7 A.M. We'd exercise, have a few laughs, then go out for coffee. That way, I'd start the day with some companionship."

Following Ginger's gaze, I watch the women as first one, then another leans forward to make a point, admit a weakness, or tell a story—then leans back to deliver a pithy comment, crack a joke, or give someone some straightforward advice.

"It's been a big help," Ginger admits. "They're great."

Later I ask Tiffany Dewees, the club's owner, about the group. She chuckles. "They're like a big group of sisters. They have their issues, just like any family, but they take care of one another. Sometimes they go out for dinner, and when one of the group became a grandmother, they threw her a baby shower. When another woman started chemo, everybody sent her a card the same day."

Tiffany nods toward the group of laughing women surrounding Ginger and lowers her voice. "They organized this whole thing just for Ginger. It's the first anniversary of her husband's death—and they didn't want her to be alone."

Watching as one chattering woman slid in beside Ginger and another sat down across from her, I realized the gift these women offered. Without making a fuss, they let her sit quietly within the circle of their caring. She didn't have to say a word or lift a hand. She could simply drink in their strength, absorb their energy, and heal under their loving smiles.

I caught Tiffany's eye, and we both smiled.

Women are such a blessing.

A Good Community

What one determined woman and an entire town can do.

Slipping slowly through the trees from one pool of early morning sunlight to another, I guided the Prius along a dirt road and down the mountain into town.

The sun had just spilled over the mountain peak above me, and the western slope on which I traveled was caught in that exquisite moment between the lingering coolness of a summer night and the heat of a summer day.

Maples, oaks, and elderberry sparkled with moisture overhead, and wisps of an early morning mist lingered among the wildflowers lining the road. I was on my way to swim morning laps at the local high school, and if I wanted a good workout, I didn't have time to linger.

Ten minutes later I approached the town of Bristol and slowed. Old-fashioned gas lamps, white Victorian houses, and yellow clapboard buildings with elaborately carved and painted trim line the main street. American flags, draped from the lampposts from Memorial Day until Labor Day, hang motionless in the stillness. Huge pots of flowers sit beside doorways, and every color of petunia imaginable wildly spills over the edges of window boxes from one end of town to the other.

It's rare to see the town without people gathered in twos and threes up and down the street, talking about everything from building permits and gas prices to their aunt Emily's back pain, the library's book sale, or their daughter's trip to Norway.

Already a guy in jeans, workboots, and a Boston Red Sox cap is crossing the street with a cup of coffee in his hand.

Pretty soon, everyone else will be moving as well. In an hour my friend Sherry will open her restaurant. Across the street, my friend Cindy will unlock the door of her office-services shop and her dog Casey will jump up into the low window display to keep an eye out for her favorite customers. A couple of hours later my friend Jan will open her gift shop, and next door her neighbor Bonita will open Vermont HoneyLights, the candlemaking shop she and a group of friends started several years ago.

Thinking of the candlemaker makes me smile. Bonita is a pistol. Tiny, full of laughter, intelligence, and funny one-liners, Bonita has a warm energy that gets things done. When her twin granddaughters were born in 1989, one of them, Kayla, had cystic fibrosis (CF), the most prevalent genetic disease in the country. But money for research was tight, and only a few guys who worked in deep science really talked about it. Back then, all that most of us knew was that CF produced a sticky mucus that clogged the airways of its victims and killed them by age 12. We didn't know that a simple blood test before pregnancy could determine whether or not a man or woman had the gene that could cause it.

It's not an easy disease. But Bonita vowed that it wasn't going to ruin Kayla's life. So she and her husband, Dave Bedard, drew together a group of family, friends, and neighbors to raise money for CF research.

The first year, they held a walk-a-thon through the town and raised $2,500.

Today, a decade or so later, what is now called the "Three-Day Stampede for the Cure"—it's a stampede because everyone is in too much of a hurry for a cure to walk—has literally taken over the town for one long weekend every summer. Not only is there a "stampede" through town, but there's a chicken barbecue, silent auction, raffle, bingo, bake sale, a craft and flea market, and a lawn sale at the town rec field with 15 huge tents full of donated clothes, bikes, books, food, and just about anything somebody might need. One hundred percent of everything is donated, and 100 percent of the money raised goes to the Cystic Fibrosis Foundation—over $600,000 to date.

Looking at the candle store, I realize that it's amazing what one determined woman can do—especially when she's blessed with the support of a small town that has its priorities straight.

The guy with the coffee has just fired up his truck, so I offer up a silent prayer of thanks for the fact that I live here, and I turn toward the high school.

There's no cure yet for CF. But research thus far has enabled kids like Kayla to live longer, healthier lives.

This year Kayla will celebrate her 17th birthday.

By rights it should be in the middle of the village green—surrounded by the entire town.

The Garden Club

As weeds are pulled, vegetables harvested, and memories shared, the boundaries between us blur.

As I pulled into the rehab center's parking lot, the late afternoon sun began to descend beyond the neighboring Adirondacks and bathe the center's low California-style building in a warm glow. Birds fluttered and twittered among trees lining the walkways, a few seagulls in need of a GPS adjustment strutted back and forth in front of the doors, and a half-dozen women of multiple generations sat and talked comfortably on benches.

Swinging open my car's back hatch, I grabbed the purple trug loaded with my gardening tools—a sharp trowel, leather gloves, three types of clippers, plus a bottle of sunscreen—and headed toward the doors.

It was Tuesday afternoon, and, as I had all summer, I was here to hang out with several elderly gardeners who had been sidelined by various injuries and illnesses.

Each has serious disabilities that can make movement difficult, speech halting, or thought slow, and most use wheelchairs or walkers. But each also has an abiding passion for the soil, a deep love of anything that grows, and more botanical knowledge in their gnarled fingers than I—despite four months of classes with soil scientists at the University of Vermont—could possibly cram into my brain cells.

I breezed through the doors, squirted a waterless cleaner on my hands, and headed for the activities room.

blessed

"Well! Finally!" boomed out one of the gardeners as she impatiently wheeled to meet me.

I chuckled. "Yep—finally. Are you guys ready to weed?"

The group, three women and one man, plus another volunteer Master Gardener like me, nod their heads and slowly but eagerly begin to edge their wheelchairs toward a double door that opens onto a courtyard. Most are mobile, but a couple of them need a helping push.

"Here," I say to my friend Sarah, handing her my trug. "What if you carry the trug and I push the chair? These tools are heavy."

She nods her agreement. "Just don't forget to bring a basket," she cautions. "I want to get the last of those cucumbers before Ted does."

Once in the courtyard, Ted pushes himself over to the fountain to watch the water while the rest of the group meanders along paths lined by lush borders of evergreens and perennials. Russian sage, a tall, delicate plant with lavender flowers that scents the courtyard whenever a leaf is gently brushed by a reverent hand, is the group's favorite. The sunny yellow black-eyed Susan is a close runner-up, and Jean, a former teacher, pauses to tell us of the ones that grew in her backyard back home. Then Sarah tells us about the peonies she grew beside her front steps, and Jane relates the time her girls picked every rose in her garden for a doll's wedding.

The women laugh. Each flower seems to remind the wheelchair-bound gardeners of stories they want to share. The coreopsis that grew so tall it hid the back steps. The ivy that ate a garage. The begonias that took down a window box.

Bit by bit, as we pull weeds, harvest vegetables, and cut back straggling vines, garden problems are spotted and solved, helping hands reach from one wheelchair to another, memories are shared, and the boundaries between us blur.

We are so blessed.

Dinner by the Lake

It's not easy to build strong friendships in a world that delivers
everything else in the flash of a cursor.

Sitting at a sunny table on the side porch of the Inn at Shelburne Farms, my friend Dolores leaned back in her chair with a sigh of satisfaction. She had just finished an exquisite dinner of freshly picked greens and vegetables, crowned by a lovely haddock. And as she picked up her coffee and looked out over the rolling lawns toward Lake Champlain and the Adirondacks beyond, I could tell that she was feeling more relaxed than when she'd arrived.

"How are the girls?" I asked.

"Oh! I forgot to tell you!" she replied, and launched into a story about grown-up daughters Kara and Kim. Kim, a diplomat's wife and new mom in Armenia, and Kara, a graphic designer in New York, were the light of Dolores's life. If the girls were fine, so was she. If they weren't, well, if they weren't, there would be a constant tightness to Dolores's jaw as she remained vigilant, cell in hand, ready to take action. Whatever they needed, she would make sure it happened. It was who she was.

But today all was well, and, as we sat comfortably on the old brick terrace under a striped awning, our conversation drifted from children to books, art and music, then back to books again. Both of us lived and breathed the printed word, whether it was printed on a page or illuminated on a screen. In fact, we had met 24 years before at a publishing company. Dolores was the copy chief, and I was a newbie book editor. It was her job to assign me a copy editor for my first project, and she had invited me to lunch to size me up.

"My job," she had begun carefully as she picked up her sandwich, "is to serve the reader by making sure the book adheres to the rules of the Chicago Manual and our house style."

I picked up a carrot from my salad. *"My* job," I had countered as I looked her straight in the eye, "is to push the envelope on those rules so that the reader absorbs information more effectively."

We looked at one another in amazement. We had each actually met someone who took verbs, voice, and mood seriously. In a cafeteria surrounded by authors and editors, it wasn't, unfortunately, all that common.

"You," I pointed at her with a carrot, "are the Vestal Virgin of the English language. You're supposed to uphold its traditions in grammar, usage, and style. It's your job to tell me when I've pushed the envelope too far."

"I," the carrot swung toward my chest, "am supposed to invent new ways to use that language so the reader can absorb more information with less effort."

The two of us looked at each other in delight, and off we went— two women completely committed to good writing, good books, and a friendship that has now spanned nearly a quarter century.

It's not easy to build strong friendships in a fast-paced world that delivers everything but babies in the flash of a cursor. In a culture that has everyone on speed dial, communication becomes too brief—too inconsequential—for the exploration and depth friendship requires.

Yet Dolores and I have managed to challenge that reality. Not that we had a lot of time to hang out. We were both working moms, wives, and dedicated professionals with responsibilities for older relatives. But little by little, a late lunch here, a 4 P.M. coffee there, we built a relationship that has nurtured us both.

When I was trying to figure out how to save enough money to put my then-10 year-old through college, it was Dolores who suggested the strategy and the investments that would do it.

When Dolores was trying to cope with two bright, independent girls during their teenage years, I was the one who validated her decisions and supported her choices.

When I was dealing with a crazy, incompetent boss who tried to cover her own mistakes by hanging them around the necks of her team, Dolores listened to my howls of frustration, shared my indignation, and helped me figure out what to do.

And when Dolores decided she'd have to leave her marriage to become the woman she was meant to be—a woman who appreciated good art, loved good music, reveled in good books, and traveled the world—I celebrated the courage it took to gently disengage and move forward.

Getting together over the past few years has been hard as each of us moved to different states and our careers have moved in different directions. Dolores travels to London, Washington, Frankfurt, Istanbul, New York, and any other place her business—and her sense of adventure—takes her. I nestle here in my beloved cottage high in the mountains of Vermont, reluctant to leave my dogs and gardens. But once or twice a year, we find a weekend, a concert, and a beautiful, exquisite restaurant.

Now, watching my friend sparkle as she listens to Mozart from an orchestra on the inn's south porch, I realize that I am thrice blessed. Once for her friendship. Once for her presence.

Once for who she is.

A Woman's Strength

When a mother prepares to die, her daughters hold her hand.

Looking across the table at my friend Jane as she samples a glass of blueberry wine from a vineyard down in the valley, I listen as she reminisces about her mom.

Mary had been a special woman. She had raised five spirited children on her husband's schoolteacher salary, nurtured the creative sparks within each, and encouraged each to follow a different drummer.

But several years ago, Mary had been diagnosed with colon cancer and given three months to live.

"It was a shock," admits Jane now as she sips her wine and looks out over the woods that surround my cottage.

She and her brothers and sisters, all adults and most with children of their own, were devastated. One lived nearby in Connecticut, while the other four were scattered across Colorado, Pennsylvania, and Massachusetts. All were busy with careers and had serious responsibilities both at home and in the workplace.

"But my mom wanted to die at home," remembers Jane. "So my sister Chris and I decided to make it happen."

Chris, a teacher, took a leave of absence and moved back home to do the heavy lifting. She would assume her mother's day-to-day 24-hour care, interface with the hospice nurses and doctors, administer medication, and make sure her mother got the best possible care and the easiest possible death.

Jane, a corporate art director for a publishing company in Pennsylvania, would work the 60 hours a week her job demanded between Monday and Friday, then drive five hours to Connecticut every Friday night to relieve Chris. On Sunday night at 6 P.M., she'd drive home, fall into bed, then get up Monday morning and start over.

"It was grucling," she admits. "Remember when I fell on the ice in our driveway and broke my leg?" She laughs. "I lay there in the dark until someone found me!"

Remember? How could I forget?

Jane is one of my closest friends, and every Monday afternoon at 4 P.M. we would meet in the company cafeteria to talk about our work and jack up our energy with coffee. We needed to churn out a significant amount of work before we left every night at 7 or 8, but by 4 o'clock our brain cells were dead. So coffee became our drug of choice. When the company installed an espresso bar, we were overjoyed. A double espresso could keep us clicking until 10 P.M., which meant that we'd even have the energy to hang out with our kids when we finished work.

It was not a healthy lifestyle for either of us. We weren't working for glory, just to support our families. Fortunately, we were both married to artists who worked from home. The guys were there after school for the kids, and although we never knew who would be covered with mud, paint, blood, or the gritty dust of an in-progress sculpture, the fact was that the guys could handle soccer practice, grocery shopping, and tussling boys with casual competence and were actually able to put together some decent meals.

In any case, possibly because of the incredible care Jane and Chris gave their mother, Mary lasted 18 months—a whole year longer than her doctors had predicted.

It was hard. But when the end came, Mary was not alone. She was loved, she was cherished, she was honored, she was in her own bed, and she was surrounded by her entire family.

As for Jane and Chris, I don't know two finer women on the planet. As women always do, they swallowed their tears, rolled up their sleeves, and did what was needed.

Looking across the table at Jane as she puts down her wineglass and laughs, I feel blessed just to be in their presence.

The Gruesome Twosome Ride Again

No husbands. No kids. No dogs. Just us, hundreds of miles of beach, the Atlantic ocean, spring sunshine, lots of seafood, a bottle of wine, and a gazillion pieces of vanilla saltwater taffy with which to ruin our teeth.

Stepping out of the F-terminal onto the sidewalk at Philadelphia international Airport, I studied the cars whizzing by in the spring sunshine, looking for a huge blue I'm-a-mom-I-can-carry-the-whole-team van with a redhead at the wheel.

Almost on cue, my cell phone launched into Beethoven's 9th. I flipped it open.

"I'm just entering the terminal throughway," said my friend Deb into my ear. "Where are you?"

"In front of the baggage area. At the curb—I see you!"

Practically leaping into the street in excitement, I waved to the van moving into the right lane. Ninety seconds later I was in the vehicle hugging the stuffing out of my best friend.

Debbie Childers and I have been friends since our two boys met in preschool some—I cannot believe this—28 years ago. We swapped kids, borrowed tool-handy husbands, spent summers surrounded by wild munchkins at the community pool, took our kids strawberry picking, pumpkin hunting and sledding. And every Christmas we built gingerbread houses at Deb's with an entire neighborhood's worth of small people.

"Mrs. Mi*chaud*," she would say severely as my gingerbread dough crumbled yet again, "that is NOT the way we do gingerbread!"

"Mrs. *Chil*ders," I'd reply dismissively, "you're just TOO picky!"

We homeroom-momed, ran school fundraising projects, guided school principals in the right direction, and lobbied the school board with our views on serious issues. I'm still not sure if it was us or a school board member who, after I incredulously asked the entire board, "Are you saying that you're putting your concern for insurance issues *AHEAD* of our children's safety on the playground?" labeled the two of us the "Gruesome Twosome."

Eventually, as college, jobs, girlfriends, and a move half a state away pulled the boys apart, Debbie and I still managed to stay close. We took each other to lunch on our birthdays and tried to meet for an occasional weekend.

Those weekends have been rare. Last year, after having seen her only once—in an ER for six hours, for Pete's sake!—I had promised her that come hell or high water *this* year I'd fly to her home near Philadelphia and the two of us would head to the beach for a girlfriend getaway.

No husbands. No kids. No dogs. Just us, hundreds of miles of beach, the Atlantic ocean, spring sunshine, lots of seafood, a bottle of wine, and a gazillion pieces of vanilla saltwater taffy with which to ruin our teeth. Maybe we'd read, for sure we would walk on the beach, but mostly we would talk.

We would make sense of our lives. We would detect patterns, discuss nuance, spot missed opportunities, recalculate costs, examine family relationships, chart new directions, and explore everything under the sun.

And when we were done, we'd remember that—particularly when the ground was shifting under our feet and the world as we knew it was disappearing—sharing time with a friend was one way we'd survive.

We are so blessed.

The Lady's Song

"Why is it taking so long?" said my mother-in-law in weak frustration. "Why don't I just go?"

The bulky Irishman in jeans and windbreaker filled the doorway to my mother-in-law's condominium, almost blocking out the weak spring sunshine that had finally emerged from days of rain.

Wordlessly, he held out a permit that allowed me to park steps from my mother-in-law's garden. "Thank you," I responded, accepting the permit. Then, peering up at him more closely, "I know you, don't I?"

"Yeah. I'm Mickey." He struggled for words. "I didn't know she was sick."

"Oh, Mickey, I'm so sorry." I held the door wide. "Please, come in."

Mickey and I had met several times over the years. As a young man barely in his twenties, he had joined the maintenance staff at Oak Hill, the condominium complex near Philadelphia to which my mother- and father-in-law had retired. He'd quickly become a favorite—always teasing my father-in-law that he was going to steal his wife, Alyce, and take her dancing. My mother-in-law would giggle delightedly, and my father-in-law would chuckle and look proudly at his vivacious, dark-eyed wife.

Thirty years later, Mickey was in charge of managing Oak Hill's acres of prime real estate, my father-in-law was gone, and my mother-in-law, at age 101, had embarked on her final journey.

"Would you like to see her?" I asked Mickey.

He nodded, and walked quickly down the hall toward her bedroom.

The morning sun filtered through the sheer drapes she had chosen long ago, and the room's rich greens and yellows reflected the happy, bright colors that had always appealed to her. Photos of family were on a chest, paintings by French street painters and her son adorned the walls, and piles of the silver and gold rings and bracelets she loved were scattered across every surface. A tv constantly tuned to CNN for the latest political news was on an old end table, close enough for the diminutive figure in the bed to keep an eye on Wolf Blitzer. A remote-control device was firmly clutched in her right hand in case he failed to do his job.

Mickey dropped to his knees beside the bed. "Hey, doll," he said softly. "I thought we were going dancing."

My mother-in-law moved her half-open eyes away from the television. "What? Who…Oh, *Mickey,*" she said, recognizing her beloved friend.

She dropped the remote and reached up to him with thin age-spotted arms, her fingers still circled with rings and her wrist cuffed with a huge silver bracelet. Mickey captured her delicate fingers in his big hands. "I though you wanted to waltz," he said, gently squeezing her fingers. She smiled and, holding tight to his hands, proceeded to tell him how much she loved him, how much she appreciated all his help over the years, how much their relationship had meant to her. He told her that it had been a pleasure, that he loved her—and was still ready to take her dancing when she was ready.

The love emanating from the two of them was palpable. Cells, beepers, and pagers crackled from Mickey's belt, demanding his attention. But Alyce didn't notice, and neither did he. Eventually, he left, knowing it would be for the last time.

Later that afternoon, my mother-in-law leaned against me as I gently stroked back her hair and rubbed her shoulders. "Why is it taking so *long?*" she said in weak frustration. "Why don't I just *go?*"

I chuckled. My mother-in-law has always had control issues, and she couldn't understand why, now that she'd decided she was ready to die, it didn't happen immediately. "I don't know, Lady," I said gently. "This isn't up to you. Maybe God thinks there's something left for you to teach us."

She thought about that for a minute, then nodded her head in weary acceptance. A few minutes later she was asleep.

In the days that have followed, she has woken only for brief periods—to tell her youngest daughter how much she loves her, to beam with pride at her granddaughter Rachael, to tell her grandson Matthew what joy he has brought to her life, and—amazingly—to weakly sing an entire chorus of a coloratura's aria—in Italian—with her opera-loving eldest daughter.

Today, as I watch yet another morning sun wash through her room, she breathes quickly as she sleeps. Tomorrow, or the day after, or the day after that, she'll leave. But she will have taught us her greatest lesson: that we are loved. That we are blessed. That we are connected, one to the other, by a tiny woman who can hit the high notes in the darkest moments of life.

A Vermont Season

Cards, gifts, wreaths, cookies, and a woman who loves it all.

It was the day before Thanksgiving, and I was already on the phone with Cheryl Werner, co-owner of Werner's Tree Farm near Middlebury, Vermont.

"OK, here's what I need this year," I began after we'd exchanged our yearly so-what-have-you-been-up-tos. Pulling out my list, I check off each item one at a time.

"Two 18-inch balsam wreaths with plaid ribbons—one wired to tie to the car's grill, the other with just a loop to hang on the back door."

"Got it."

"Three mixed-green garlands—two 22-footers to tie around the front door and porch railings; one 24-footer to frame the door of my church."

I can hear Cheryl scribbling. "Three garlands—check."

"One 24-inch swag, mixed greens, juniper berries, no ribbon, for the front door. That long plaid ribbon I have will last another year," I add, "so just leave me a place to put it. How's that sound?"

"Good," Cheryl approves. "What about a few pine cones?"

"Perfect." I check off the swag.

We finalize the details of what I need and arrange for me to head over to the farm and pick everything up the following weekend.

Sitting back in my dining-room chair, a sense of contentment begins to push past my edges as I look around the cluttered table. Covered with cards, stamps, address books, recipes, ribbons, fresh-clipped pine branches from the trees that surround my cottage, gift wrap, silver bells—it's a jumble of stuff that will help me show friends, family, and neighbors how much they are loved.

The Hanukkah cards go out first, closely followed by Christmas cards and gifts that go in the mail—Lake Champlain chocolates to my friend Denise, a book to my friend Jane, wildly colored socks to my friend Debbie, some poetry to my friend Dolores.

Then I start to bake. Fragrant gingerbread people that will be tied to the Christmas tree with silky red ribbons are carefully crafted and baked, then packed into plastic containers and hidden in the back of the freezer.

Christmas cookies drizzled with almond icing are deftly tucked into colorful little packages for my husband's next run through the community as a Meals on Wheels volunteer. A second batch is prepared for the senior citizen's community supper a week before Christmas. A third is packed for the cookies-and-cider celebration after the church Christmas candlelight service.

Then a dark, rich Vermont chocolate is whipped with fresh crème from the farm down the road into chocolate mousse and tucked away in the freezer behind the summer's green beans until Christmas night. It's quickly followed by a buttery-rich pecan pie for New Year's Day that goes into the freezer incognito—usually disguised in layered tinfoil as a quiche, which no one in my family would touch with a 10-foot pole.

Looking out the window as snow begins to pile up around my cottage, I pick up the first card to address—and realize that from Thanksgiving to New Year's my whole life will be focused on doing a zillion small things for family, friends, neighbors, and people I don't even know.

Somehow, I just can't stop smiling.

My Secret Garden

Staying connected to our kids is tough—especially when they're busy adults with lives of their own.

Pushing open the vintage French doors with their lovely old beveled glass, I stepped out of the 1920s Hollywood bungalow and into a secret garden.

Sheltered by an 80-foot-tall sycamore and surrounded by jasmine hedges, Chinese elm, stone walls thick with ivy, a tumble-down garage covered with bougainvillea, and a soaring stand of bamboo, the garden was a magical space of dappled California sunlight and green growing things. Had a unicorn stepped out from under a tree, I wouldn't have been surprised.

"Mom?"

In the doorway behind me, my son Matthew appeared.

"Wow! This is so you!"

Catching sight of a hummingbird among the jasmine, I agreed. Beds of budding roses, lush orchids, miniature iris, and other perennials looked familiar, but dozens of others—both in beds, bordering the garden, and tumbling out of pots—were just different enough from their cousins in my yard back in Vermont that all I could do was guess at their names.

"You want me to set up your chair before I go?"

Turning back to answer, I was overwhelmed with how much I love this incredible person. A screenwriter, Matthew had moved to an apartment here three years ago in Beachwood Canyon, a slash through the

Hollywood Hills from downtown Hollywood to the San Fernando Valley. Craftsman bungalows and cliff-clinging stucco houses are tucked among the Chinese elm, bamboo, and eucalyptus that cover the canyon's steep sides, while narrow lanes twist and turn between them.

"Could you put the chair by the jasmine?" I asked as I inhaled the scents of damp earth and flowers. "I can work out here in the garden with my laptop."

He looked at me knowingly and began unfolding the chair. "Uh-huh. Work." He chuckled. "I'll be inside."

For my son, the move to Beachwood Canyon has been a good one. The canyon has been a secluded retreat for artists, writers, musicians, and serious film people since the 1920s. It's minutes from major studios and industry meeting places, but here there are no celebrities, bars, or paparazzi—just a village market, a community coffee shop, and people who walk their dogs and stop to chat with neighbors sitting out on their porches after dinner.

On the edge of a city characterized by 10-story movie posters hung from buildings, wannabe celebrities hustling for connections, and billboards touting liposuction as the way to a perfect life, Beachwood Canyon is an oasis of sanity that grounds its residents in what's real.

Sitting down in my chair to study the garden, I thought about living here for the next few weeks. My bungalow was two blocks from Matthew's apartment, which meant that he and his dog, Frankie, could pop in for breakfast or dinner whenever they pleased. I had rented the bungalow from opera singer Suzan Hanson—a friend based in Los Angeles—to hole up and work on a book that my publisher wanted next month. But I had also rented it because I wanted time with my son.

Finding time and ways to stay connected to our kids is tough—particularly when the kids are busy adults with lives of their own. If they're just down the street, around the corner, or in the next town, it's at least possible to lure them home with a good pot roast. But when they move clear across the country, across an ocean, or around the world—well, then it takes some thought.

It's not that we don't stay in touch, I realized as I caught sight of Matthew at a window inside the bungalow, talking on his cell phone. Tweeting, e-mail, webcams, and cell phones keep us aware of the day-to-day events in each other's lives. But the technology lacks the deeper communication of touch, the sense of connection—that simple awareness of what another human being is feeling when he's standing right beside you.

Watching Matthew pace back and forth as he talks, earnestly trying to express himself to someone he clearly cares about, I begin to wonder if the very devices that are supposed to bring us together are actually holding us apart. Is it possible they create an artificial intimacy that sabotages the very closeness we're trying to maintain?

Yikes.

Getting up and walking back into the bungalow, I'm glad I came to the canyon. The greatest gift of my life is here. And his presence is a blessing.

Ted's Gloves

All across America, our old folks are disappearing into retirement communities. What have we lost?

When 88-year-old Elise stood up after church, looked lovingly around the circle of dear sweet faces gathered around the room, and said, "Oh, it's *so* good to be back," there wasn't a member of that circle who wasn't equally grateful to have her standing among us.

Four years ago Elise had moved from her home on a nearby lake to a retirement community about 30 miles away. Our church—a simple country church of 15 to 20 regular attenders—missed her like crazy. Every Sunday morning for what seemed to be whole lifetimes, each of us had looked forward to her loving regard and, not infrequently, a good dose of her common sense. Our children wiggled with delight under her enthusiastic appreciation of their Sunday school projects and thrived under her steadfast encouragement to be all that God intended.

Every summer we gathered at the home she and her husband, Ted—gone many years now—had built on a nearby lake. We swam, canoed, stuffed ourselves silly with her brownies, and celebrated our community. Every winter Ted loaded up the 200-year-old woodstove that heated our church, as we gathered around and told her our stories, and listened for her confirmation that the complex paths we walked through the world were indeed the right ones.

Young or old, we could each turn to her with the big questions of life. Whether it was about careers, difficult relationships, or prayer vigils

blessed

on the village green, Elise—who had worked for years in the administration of a school that focused on international affairs—would always ask those probing questions that helped us move to a right decision.

But several years ago Elise began to travel that uneven road of forgetfulness, confusion, and anxiety toward dementia. Its onset was rapid; its progress unrelenting. In what seemed to be no time at all, her life became a list of things she'd lost. Her ability to drive. Her garden. Her daffodils. Us.

When she saw us, she wept for joy. When she was away from us, well, her family reported that the disease was progressing—robbing her of joy and energy. Twice the entire group drove to her retirement community en mass, to worship with her there, but the details for scheduling the visits were a bit overwhelming for our aging parishioner. So we contented ourselves with her presence on those occasions when her children—who attended a different church—could pick her up and bring her to us.

Finally, last year the family hired a companion to drive Elise to and from church every week. Not that she realizes how often she comes. In fact, every week she thinks she's been away for a long while and is just now returning. "It's so good to be back," she says, her blue eyes luminous with joy. And each of us nods our head in agreement, puts an arm around her thin shoulders, and gives her a tender hug. All across the country, men and women like Elise are disappearing into retirement residences and robbing our communities of their love and wisdom. We are deeply grateful to have retrieved this one.

Her eyes roam over the loving faces that surround her and light on a pair of tattered blue gloves dropped on the hearth beside the woodstove. "Oh! There are Ted's gloves!" she says in delight.

They will be there forever.

Auntie's Dilemma

How do you tell a 91-year-old lady who has worked hard all her life that 40 percent of her life savings have disappeared?

As snow piled up outside my cottage, I nudged our intrepid Westie away from the woodstove, where he was in danger of singeing a paw, and bent down to hand my elderly aunt a plate of lemon cookies and a cup of her favorite English tea. She accepted the plate with a murmured thanks, then looked up at me sharply, a moment of awareness pushing through the Alzheimer's that normally scrambles her thoughts and causes great gaping holes in her memory.

"Am I all right?"

The cup rattled in its saucer, earning me a displeased look, but I couldn't help it. Since we'd been talking a few minutes before about her annual church tithe, I knew she wasn't referring to her health. She was referring to her money. And I really didn't want to answer the question. How do you tell a 91-year-old lady who has worked hard all her life that 40 percent of her life savings have disappeared?

"Am I all right?" she repeated.

I hesitated as a vision of her last financial statement flashed through my head. "Yeah—unless you decide to live to be a thousand years old," I told her lightly. "Then we're in trouble."

"Oh. Good." The mists swirled back across her eyes, and for once, I was grateful that she would not remember today. Nor would she remember my answer, which had come pretty close to violating the

"Thou shalt not" dictum that I obeyed even when my mother-in-law asked me if she looked younger than her sister-in-law.

Not that I lied to my aunt. That's not who I am or the way I work. I respect my aunt, and I understand that my fiduciary responsibility as her legal decision maker dictates that I keep her informed. So I've kept her aware of the crazy way the American economy has behaved for the past six months, and the fact that she, like almost every other American, has lost money. I just haven't gone into detail.

I mean, *how* would I explain to a 91-year-old woman that the money she had frugally tucked away for 40 years from her salary as a book-keeper has been lost by greedy bankers, unethical stockbrokers, and arrogant politicians obsessed with following an economic theory meant for a smaller nation in a simpler time? How would I explain that she has only enough money for two more years?

Yes, she'll get a small check each month from the Social Security Administration. And, yes, she'll get Medicare, although that program—with its monthly premiums, 20 percent copays, and annual deductions—is no longer the sweet deal its authors originally intended. And neither program will cover the large fees demanded by the assisted living facility that she needs.

Sighing, I sit down across from my aunt with my own tea. I have no idea how we'll pull it off, but, like families everywhere, my husband and I will bring her to live with us. I don't know who'll take care of her while my husband and I work, or if in fact we'll be able to work when the Alzheimer's keeps both her and us up half the night. I don't even know if we'll *have* a home by the time markets stop crashing, jobs stop disappearing, and politicians stop playing games.

One thing I do know, however, is that when the chips are down, history teaches that Americans will do two things:

One, we will care for one another. Not just niece for aunt, or daughter for mother, or son for father. But neighbor for neighbor, friend for friend, stranger for stranger. We will do it because, in the United States of America, that's who we are.

Two, we will pray. From the diversity of our many faiths, we will open ourselves to what God has to say, listen carefully, then lift up our voices and pray for those who are poor and suffering, those who are old and in need, those who have led us into this dark time.

"Am I all right?"

Looking over at my aunt happily sneaking the dog a cookie, I realize that I *did* tell her the truth. With all of us caring for one another and listening to God, she will be fine.

The September Garden

All around me plants were drunk on sunshine and compost.
It was something my aunt would never see.

Sitting out on the porch as the morning sun flowed over the mountaintop and through the trees that surround my cottage, I sipped a cup of coffee and watched as Rufus, the West Highland white terrier who can usually be found lying at my feet, took off across the grass to investigate the smells of last night's nocturnal visitors. Whoever my visitors had been—maybe voles, possibly a deer or bear—-Rufus's nose skimmed over the stones outlining the lavender bed, then began an intense study of the foot-high wicker fence surrounding the vegetable garden.

Oh-oh. I looked carefully at the garden, then sighed, put down my coffee, and picked up my gardening gloves and a pair of clippers from the bench. The garden looked as though it had been on a three-day bender. Tomato vines clung to their towers for support, huge leaves of winter squash tilted this way and that, and cucumbers tumbled over the willow fences, grabbed hold of the summer squash, then took off across the mulch toward the zucchini. The corn shot straight up out of what used to be the carrot patch with sweet baby corn clinging for dear life to its stalks.

In fact, looking around the clearing, I realized that although something had clearly been throwing its weight around in my garden, just about everything looked a little end of season. All around me plants leaned and lurched as though they were drunk on sunshine and compost—although the new burrow that had been dug right under the biggest winter squash showed me where the Midnight Marauder was based. Rufus looked longingly over the wicker fence at the burrow's entrance, then up at me.

"Touch it and die," I warned him. He looked quizzically at me for a moment, then lay down in the grass with his nose pressed against the fence. He knew that tone. If the burrow's residents came out for a stroll, however, he was ready.

Although it's barely September, these are the last days of summer here in the mountains. The leaves started turning two weeks ago, and even though daytime temperatures are still warm, I've already had to put a comforter on the bed. It will be another two weeks before I"ll admit that I've needed to close the bedroom windows at night—a month before the screens come down and the garden's put to bed—but suddenly I realize that I have already begun nesting.

Everywhere I turn is evidence that I've been preparing for winter. I turned 50 pounds of tomatoes into salsa, gathered kindling for the woodstove, washed all the windows, and bought enough wool at the Knits & Bolts in New Haven to make three prayer shawls for my woodstove-heated church and a lap blanket for my 92-year-old aunt. In fact, I cast on 200 stitches of maroon wool last night.

As I tie up the tomato vines and snip off suckers, I think about my aunt. She is no longer at her little apartment overlooking the lake in Shelburne. She began falling last November, and every time she hit the floor—nine times so far—the assisted living community in which she lived sent her to the hospital for X-rays. After fall number 7, doctors sent her to a rehab facility to see if its physical therapists could build up her strength.

She fell there, too, and after six weeks of exercises, the staff realized that she wouldn't improve. So she traded her walker for a wheelchair, and at a meeting of her physical therapists, speech therapists, nurse manager, social workers, and a nurse from her assisted living community, the recommendation was made that she receive long-term care.

She agreed.

I have been in tears ever since. This is not what she and I had planned. Rather, we had imagined that she would stay in her little apartment, snuggled in her wingback chair, a book in her lap, looking out the window at the lake until she dropped.

But now she can't get up out of her wheelchair anymore without help, even to get a drink of water or go to the bathroom. Worse, the forgetfulness she'd been experiencing for several years has finally and inexplicably exploded into full-blown dementia.

The dementia is killing her. An Englishwoman by birth, my aunt has adhered to a rigid code of conduct since she was born. She worked hard, attended church, respected her parents, took care of her mother after her father died, helped her sister when she needed it, and opened her home to me when, as a rebellious teen, I needed a place to get out from under my parents' tyranny for a few weeks every summer.

That's who she is. She has always done what was right and followed the rules.

So it has been a shock to watch her disintegrate into someone I only vaguely know. She delights in disarming alarms that are meant to keep her safe. She pushes people in the dining room who are in her way. She rummages through other people's drawers thinking they've stolen her stuff. She curses. She attacks her roommates. And she doesn't remember knitting the beautiful afghan at the foot of her bed.

Tears slide down my cheeks as I finish with the tomatoes and move on to the squash. But soon the garden is put to rights, the sun soothes my grief, and both Rufus and I head for the cottage. There I sit in my own wingback chair and pick up my knitting needles to stitch my aunt's blanket.

I can't stop the dementia. I can't stop her from falling. I can't make her well. But I can keep her warm, bake her treats, visit her every week, and bring her Gabby, my little French bulldog—all of which make her smile.

So today, for me, and for her, that's a blessing.

Acknowledgments

This book is the result of an amazing collaboration among an amazing group of people.

First, Texas businesswoman Diane Heavin, who, aside from being one of the most compassionate women on the planet, is also cofounder of *Curves*. Several years ago when Diane asked me to write an online column called "Blessed" for the 3 million women who were members of *Curves*, I was stunned. Today I still marvel at her courage—inspirational stories about everyday blessings on a corporate website are just not done—and I am deeply grateful. The column allowed me to initiate a conversation with women all over the world, to hear their stories, share their insights, and to be brought to a deeper, richer faith because of it. It has been one of the greatest blessings of my life, and I thank Diane from the bottom of my heart.

I am also grateful to Claire Kowalchik, the thoughtful editor who invited me, along with three other women, to develop *diane Magazine* for Rodale and brought my work to Diane's attention. Claire's focus on women and their needs has been, to borrow from an old gospel song, the wind beneath my wings. In fact, a few of the stories I wrote for the magazine—"The Secret," "Women Who Ride the Dragon," and "Swapping Fire for the Sun"—were so precious to me that, with her permission, I've included them in this book.

As for the folks at Reader's Digest, I am simply stunned by their support. Harold Clarke, who had the vision to understand that sending a book full of love and light out into the global community of women during this challenging time would provide hope and inspiration, showed an amazing courage and foresight that is sadly lacking in publishing today. And he's not bad in the author relations department either—his comment, "We love Ellen," which was relayed to me by a staff member, wedded me to Reader's Digest books forever.

But this book would simply not have happened if not for Reader's Digest's trade publishing executive editor Dolores York. It was Dolores's suggestion that I gather my "Blessed" columns into a book for Reader's Digest, and it was her enthusiasm and encouragement that allowed me to add additional articles that took the book to a whole new level. She is an author's dream. She also championed the book in-house and gave

174

me the best book team in publishing: Senior Art Director George McKeon, Copy Editor Barbara Booth, and Designer Elizabeth Tunnicliffe, who understood the heart of a blessed life and brought it to the book's cover.

Also at Reader's Digest, Marketing Director Stacey Ashton patiently answered my 1,001 e-mails about readers, markets, and digital books, then put herself on the line to make this book available to women everywhere.

Then there are all the incredible women and remarkable men who shared their hearts, their souls, their work, and their stories:

Marjorie Susman and Marian Pollack at Orb Weaver's Farm in Vermont, who showed me the possibilities of living at nature's pace.

Quaker pastor Brent Bill, executive vice president of the Center for Congregations in Indianapolis, who sees the sacred in the everyday.

Vicky Gallo and Janet Bristow, two Connecticut women who got thousands of women around the globe to pick up their knitting needles and crochet hooks to weave their prayers and yarn into shawls for those who needed comforting.

Marie Pimentel, an 80+ Wisconsin "farm girl," who taught solar cooking to thousands of women across Nigeria, Mozambique, Rwanda, and Zimbabwe.

Dorothy Selebwa, who, with the help of her faith community, rounded up children who had been orphaned by AIDS and created the Kagamega Orphans Care Centre in Kenya. Maine Quaker Suki Rice, who pulled together a base of support in the United States to help make it happen.

Carly Hodgins, the former University of Vermont food-shelf organizer, who made sure the homeless in Burlington, Vermont, got fed on weekends; social worker and pastor's wife Laurie Kroll, whose big heart is responsible for rescuing a whole village of children in Uganda; Nancy Luke and Darla Senecal, two Vermont moms who pulled together women from three counties to stitch somewhere around 4,000 dresses for girls and women orphaned or widowed by AIDS in Zambia; and Save the Children's Spee Braun and her husband, Jens, who are showing all of us how to live out our faith in a simple, giving life in upstate New York.

Scholar Cynthia Woolever, Ph.D., professor of sociology and religious organization at the Hartford Seminary, who helped me understand the evolution of faith in this country.

Silvia Jope of Old World Garden Designs, who helped me plan "my mother's garden." Holly Poulin, who showed me that it's never too late to make your dreams a reality. Weed Farm's Sue Borg, who morphs from musician to farmer and back again without losing a beat. Rita Teater, a *Curves* owner in Iowa, who is bringing common sense and a passion for thrift back into fashion. Mattie MacGreggor, a physicist turned web architect, and Marjike Niles, flight attendant, turned university fundraiser, turned Master Gardener, turned entrepreneur.

Linda Dague, Blair Hall, and Nancy Orvis, who tend the Jerusalem community with loving care. Farmer—and novelist—Eugenie Doyle, whose incredible organic produce at the Bristol farmers' market inspires me as much as the novels she writes. Dragon boat paddlers and breast cancer survivors Linda Dwyer, Mary Ann Castimore, Pam Blum, and their friend Shirley.

Tiffany Dewees, Ginger Miller, and all the caring women from the North Coventry *Curves* in Pennsylvania. Bonnie Bedard, who truly demonstrates how one woman can make a difference in her community's life. Opera singer Suzan Hanson, who created my "secret garden" in Beachwood Canyon. Judith Irven and the members of the Porter Health and Rehabilitation Center's "Garden Club."

My beloved stepmother, Edna, who held "The Secret" until I was ready to hear it. My aunt Ellen, who made me understand that wanting to feed entire football teams was normal behavior for the women in my family. My "best" friends Deb, Jane, and Dolores, who are the strongest and most caring women on the planet.

I am also deeply grateful to those friends who have shared their lives and their insights with me but who have asked me to protect their privacy by not using their real names.

And I am grateful to my faith community, members of the South Starksboro Quaker Meeting, who are woven in and out of this book just as they are in my life.

Thank you all so very, very much. I have been blessed by your care.

Ellen